D1359116

PSYCHOLOGY of
Success

DEVELOP YOUR HIDDEN POWERS

A Guidebook for Students and Educators

by
Emery Stoops
Professor Emeritus
University of Southern California

Phi Delta Kappa Educational Foundation
Bloomington, Indiana U.S.A.

Cover design by
Victoria Voelker

Phi Delta Kappa Educational Foundation
408 North Union Street
Post Office Box 789
Bloomington, IN 47402-0789
U.S.A.

Printed in the United States of America

Library of Congress Control Number 2002105071
ISBN 0-87367-839-7

To Carol, Jon, Elen, Eric,
Scott, Steven, and Kimberly,
with best wishes for great achievement.

EDITOR'S PREFACE

The first edition of *Psychology of Success* was published in 1983 by Mojave Books of Reseda, California. At that time, Emery Stoops was a youthful 80 years old. He had been an educator throughout his life: teacher, counselor, assistant principal, principal, superintendent, and college professor. Following on this successful career, he embarked on another in the insurance industry.

I had the pleasure of meeting Emery several years ago in Salt Lake City, Utah, where I and several others sat over dinner and listened to some of the highlights of his remarkable life. He regaled us with stories of his early career, of traveling for Phi Delta Kappa in the 1920s, of the advent of PDK's Hawaii chapter in the 1940s, just as reliable airplane service was beginning. It was Emery who was serving as PDK's International President in 1956, when the cornerstone was set for the association's headquarters in Bloomington, Indiana. Emery Stoops has seen and been involved in much. When it comes to success, he knows whereof he writes.

Shortly before his 99th birthday in December 2001, Emery, still vigorous and still piling up successes, presented us with a revised manuscript, which we are pleased to publish in this new edition. Emery extends his appreciation to Dr. Sir James Marks for his help in revising the manuscript of this book.

Donovan R. Walling
Director of Publications and Research
Phi Delta Kappa International

TABLE OF CONTENTS

CHAPTER ONE

How to
Recognize Success

Just what is success? Success means pleasure. Success means satisfying our needs, our wants, and our goals. But success is more than that. It is self-survival in the best possible way. Success is a sure-fire way to become happy — and to make others happy. Others? Yes! It is said, "Man is a social animal." We are born into a family, a neighborhood, a nation, and a world. Our success is tied to others; and their success is tied to us.

When Cain killed Abel, his chance of success went down with his victim, and of course Abel's chance died too. Success means betterment of self-interest and also betterment of the interests of all concerned. This means mutual winning: mutual success.

In our social mutuality, neither predator nor prey can be successful. Success means the best possible life for oneself and all others. In business the store manager must provide the highest quality at the lowest price, and customers will flock to the store. Mom and Pop Stater had a little store in Fontana, California. They knew their customers by name and served each of them, not only as customers but also as valued neighbors. They were always available for help. The Stater Brothers Chain is now one of the best inland chains in California — still advertising quality goods, plus honest service, and lower prices. J.C. Penny determined to follow the Golden Rule in his store, and it became a nationwide chain.

Success for self and others is best when based upon such mutual ethics as: service, honesty, fairness, concern . . . in effect the Golden Rule.

You can be successful as a student; you can be successful as an employee. You can be successful as a member of a family and as a citizen of your country. You can make high marks, forge a successful career, create a happy marriage, and earn a million dollars. Your success is a mirror image of your lifetime journey toward your highest dreams. Success, in other words, is the realization of your loftiest aspirations.

Then, you may ask, "Can I make my dreams come true?" The answer is simple: a resounding "Yes!" You can! This book establishes the psychological basis for success. Your happy success will be made *by you* and for all concerned.

Success Lies in Your Hidden Powers

William James wrote the first successful textbook of general psychology and attained success as "the father of American psychology." James wrote about the hidden powers within each of us that make for success. While psychologists argue over the best approach or system that is to be used to study behavior and mental activity, they agree on one point. Psychologists since the time of William James have agreed that each person has powers beyond his or her awareness. These are great reservoirs of untapped *hidden powers*. Consider a few examples.

An emotional person was so incapacitated by a psychosomatic illness that he could not lift such ordinary household items as a frying pan or an iron. He spent many of his days in bed. He had always loved working in his hobby as an amateur carpenter and was recognized as having true talent in restoring old furniture, but he was too weak to work any more with his many tools, stains, and restoration coatings. He needed a special book-holder to prop up a book so that he could read it because it was "too heavy" for him to hold for any length of time. While his worried spouse was at work one day, a short-circuit caused a fire to erupt in the attic. This weakened man jumped from bed, picked up a very heavy tool kit his wife had recently given him, and raced into the front yard before he remembered that he was too weak even to consider picking up a good-size book.

Franklin Delano Roosevelt was cut down by polio and was told by one doctor that he would be permanently bedridden, or at best he would be confined to a wheelchair, able only to engage in hobbies such as knitting and stamp-collecting. Franklin Roosevelt called forth his hidden powers to gain and hold the highest office in the land for an unprecedented four terms. He used those powers at the maximum to conquer pain and fatigue during the trials of leadership, first during the Great Depression and then, decisively, during World War II.

An Iowa farmer had a painful, incapacitating slipped disc in his back. He used levers and jacks to hoist a heavy plow while replacing a wheel. A jack crumpled and allowed the plow to fall on his small son's leg. Without thinking of his painfully sore back, this farmer lifted a 200-pound plow and pushed his son clear.

Suzy was a junior in high school. She looked upon herself as being the ugliest girl in the class. She really was! She wore a scowl, stringy hair, frown-caused wrinkles, and unkempt blouses. In September, her counselor, who was a good psychologist, complimented her on the clearness of her skin. Next, she mentioned the improved tone of Suzy's voice. Every time the counselor met this ugly duckling, she noticed and mentioned the improvements that Suzy was beginning to make. This positive approach called forth personal and social powers deeply buried in Suzy. She grew and she blossomed. When it came time to elect the Queen of the Junior-Senior Prom the next spring, who do you suppose got the most votes? Suzy!

We all have hidden powers. Call them forth, and success is within your reach.

Just What Do We Mean by Hidden Powers?

Let's get specific. We can turn again to William James. He believed that individuals have almost limitless power ready to be called forth from the subconscious mind. Later psychologists question the duality of the conscious and unconscious mind, but they agree with James that great dormant power lies deep in the human nervous system.

James and all psychologists since his time recognize the fact that problem-solving continues after you have gone to sleep or have turned your mind to entirely different subjects. Try an experiment. Work on a tough problem that just has no answer by bedtime. Something happens while you sleep. In the morning, your answer will either be there, or you can solve the problem in half the time. This phenomenon is akin to what psychologists call the "Zeigarnnik effect."

When you have a mental block and cannot recall a name, forget it for thirty minutes and the name will likely pop into your consciousness.

This delayed solution to problems and this later recall indicate that some part of your mind (call it the subconscious if you like) was working while you consciously focused attention elsewhere. This productive, subconscious working of the nervous system prompted William James to say that "we learn to skate in the summer and to swim in the winter." You have the same experience when you first try to learn touch-typing or to play a musical instrument, or when you first enroll in a self-defense course. You may fail miserably at first, but as you keep trying something happens between practice sessions. You "learn to skate" without ice.

Applied to learning to use a computer keyboard through touch-typing, your fingers learn the combination between practice sessions so that one day you start off suddenly and unexpectedly with coordinated fingers.

Keats looked upon his poetic life as a failure, with his name written merely in water rather than upon the sands of time. But one day his hidden powers guided the muse within to say, "A thing of beauty is a joy forever." Immortal lines followed, and the hidden powers within burned his name into the literary halls of fame.

Glenn Cunningham had his feet burned to stubs in Elkhart, Kansas. Because he could hardly stand with any balance, he understood why the doctor shook his head when asked if Glenn would ever again walk. But Glenn had something within him that would not give up. He could not walk, but if he ran, he could maintain balance. It is the kind of equilibrium that keeps a moving bicycle in balance and lets a stationary one fall over. So Glenn Cunningham ran to school, to the store, across the prairie, and right into the gold medal row of the world's long-distance runners.

Your own hidden powers are there. It is up to you to call them forth if you desire success. You can let these powers remain a seeping spring, or you can turn that potential into a roaring stream of achievement.

How Do Hidden Powers Work?

Your hidden powers for success lie dormant and ready, but *you* must bother to call them forth. Yes, bother! You have to want to use them. Perhaps you are a student enrolled in English, history, chemistry, and mathematics, even psychology. Try this simple device. Read over — survey — your assignment in each subject before you go to sleep. Try to anticipate the substance of each assignment. Don't bother about the answers. Just get the problems well defined in your mind. In this way, you are charting the course for tomorrow's success. While you sleep, something will happen deep in your brain. Then when you do tomorrow's work, you will find that solutions and learning come much more readily. You will be solving your problems the way that Charles A. Lindbergh solved his.

Before his historic flight to Paris and his later flight across the jungles of Brazil, Lindbergh went through every phase of his flight in his mind, down to the minutest detail. He knew that several aviators had lost their lives trying to fly across the jungles of the Amazon. They had become lost and never were heard from again. Lindbergh studied his charts thoroughly, calculating every possible updraft and downdraft, every squall, every turbulence. He stamped into his mind every feature of the forest terrain below so that he knew at all times just where he was and what aerial control was needed. In short, Lindbergh called on his hidden powers to help him achieve success.

When you, as a student, anticipate (imagine) in complete detail, tomorrow's hurdles in English composition, chemical experiments, a segment of history, or a theorem in geometry, you will find that the work is half done before you even start. Release your hidden powers as a student, and you can easily rise from a C to a B, or from a B to an A.

TIPS FOR SUCCESS

- Start to make use of your untapped mental potential.
- Be optimistic and enthusiastic.
- See problems as opportunities.
- Get rid of the "I can'ts" in your thoughts, actions, and speech.
- Believe in the powerful forces of faith and hope.

The first step in solving a problem is to define it. It is important for all of us — whether students or not — first to define our targets, instead shooting arrows in all directions at once. Lindbergh knew exactly where he was going and precisely the best possible strategies for getting there. First, and foremost, *aim for the stars*! As Browning wrote, "A man's reach should exceed his grasp, or what's a heaven for?" When you have determined your greatest desires in life, focus your energy straight as an arrow and work tirelessly toward those worthwhile goals. Your hidden powers will give you strength to move a little closer each day.

Thomas Alva Edison is an example of another person who first worked out his inventions in his mind. He would read everything written on a subject, such as the recording of the human voice. This shook awake his hidden powers and put them to work. Then he started where others had left off. The next step was to imagine the final outcome and keep all of his powers directed to the realization of the final invention until it was complete.

Edison's hidden powers flared to illuminate new laws of nature, to reveal new combinations of mechanical principles, and to spot unused methods for completion — and think of what he accomplished!

Closely allied to Edison's technique is the power of prayer. For many centuries both clerics and laymen have recognized that through prayer the "impossible just takes a little longer." The ancients felt that if a man prayed for yonder mountain to be dumped into the sea, it could be done. It just took a praying man with faith enough to make a bulldozer, a mechanical monster that would chew up bite after bite of yonder mountain.

A number of students in a small Christian academy in West Virginia were failing algebra and Latin. They decided to pray for passing grades. Through prayer, these students concentrated upon removal of their own learning roadblocks and upon ways to arrive at their goal of subject mastery. They were calling upon powers from that inexhaustible well that William James had discovered. Call it what you will, their efforts led them to better study habits and to longer hours of improved concentration. And the end of a six-week experiment, except for one case, all of these former failures were making commendable marks.

The use of prayer-concentration-imagination — in short, the use of your hidden powers — is like trying to beach a boat. The use of these techniques will not pull the shore to the boat, but you will land your foundering craft by virtue of your hidden powers, operating within a universal scheme. Your hidden powers point the way.

Hidden Powers in Religion

Through the centuries, men and women have credited God for their miracles of success. Whether God comes down personally to lead the way or whether He has implanted in the neural sinews of people the capacity for success is rather beside the point. With insights furnished by psychology, we have a better idea as to how success takes place and how to make the process work even better.

An example of the release of hidden powers happened in Garden Grove, California. A young preacher by the name of Robert H. "Bob" Schuller began his ministry in Saturday's passion pit, a drive-in theater. His goal was to build one of the greatest churches in the Western world under the faith-slogan, "It's possible." Reverend Schuller (later Dr. Schuller) inspired every member of his church; he gave them new faith and hope. He kept telling them, "It's possible, it's possible, it's possible."

Starting at the age of twenty-eight in 1955 with $500 in his pocket and millions in his hidden powers of faith, he spoke from the roof of a snack bar to curious families in 50 cars and got $83 for his first offering. His self-image was strong, and his goals had no limits. It could be done. It had to be done by the power of *possibility thinking*.

Dr. Schuller's snack-bar pulpit was eventually replaced with a 14-story church and tower, topped by a 90-foot cross, where 10,000 persons sat in the pews, in cars, on the lawn, and in overflow rooms to hear him preach each Sunday. His possibility thinking drew so heavily upon his hidden powers that he inspired people in his "Hour of Power" program, which eventually was transmitted over 140 radio and television stations and reached millions. He has published many books, and his syndicated column has appeared in 750 newspapers. His program went beyond the usual, with special attention given to seniors, women, single persons, youth, and all who needed counsel. He conducted visitations, seminars, 24-hour telephone counseling, correspondence with thousands, worldwide classes in church leadership training; and he offered an outstretched invitation to every needy soul nationally and internationally.

Hidden powers, which possibility thinking called forth, cried out for even greater accomplishments. In every age, people have expressed beauty and magnificence in places of worship. Dr. Schuller's "possible" dream came true with the completion of the "Crystal Cathedral." At a cost of more than $4,000,000, the all-glass "Crystal Cathedral" is larger than Notre Dame of Paris and can seat more than four thousand worshipers.

Robert H. Schuller has proved that "it's possible." Hidden powers drawn out by possibility thinking have made for him and his followers a success that seems to have no limits.

Both fact and legend have been built upon the release of hidden powers. Boys and girls, men and women, have become famous because they were successful *beyond belief*. Consider such examples as Alexander, who designed the Greek Phalanx; George Washington at Valley Forge; Clara Barton founding the American Red Cross; the Pilgrims at Plymouth Rock; David before Goliath; Neil Armstrong on the moon; Marie Curie discovering radium; George Washington Carver in science; and the Wright Brothers at Kittyhawk. History is crammed with those who released great hidden powers.

Myths and legends abound with imaginative successes that also urge us to tap our hidden powers. Jack and the Beanstalk, the labors of Hercules, and the flights of Peter Pan fire the imagination with what could happen with the release of almost limitless potential. The imaginative stories of Jules Verne, who actually predicted the modern submarine, could well have ended with Reverend Schuller's slogan, "It's Possible."

Hidden Powers and You

You may be a student at the elementary, secondary, or college level. You may be an adult growing soybeans in Illinois, oranges in California, or cotton in South Carolina. Maybe you are using a computer, driving a truck, or seining for shrimp in the Gulf. Maybe you're a peace officer, or a teacher. Whatever you are doing, you can do it better.

By calling upon your hidden powers, you can remain in your present job and improve. You can use that position to advance to the next step in your company or organization. Or you can prove to yourself that you can succeed in several different areas of work.

Never limp along on the crutch of excuses. Don't blame your supervisor, your co-workers, or the government. Erase failure from your job vocabulary. True, you will make mistakes, but these are necessary steps to success. When someone said, "Mr. Edison, we're sorry you've failed again to make a light bulb," he retorted, "Failed nothing! I've found five hundred ways it can't be done!" Be positive, face the future, trust your hidden powers, and you can succeed.

We are all masters of our own destinies. Choose carefully a worthwhile goal in life, use your hidden powers, and you can accomplish what idlers only dream in their wildest flights of fancy.

Things to Do

This chapter has introduced the concept of hidden powers. Following are some activities related to this concept and how to tap it for success.

1. List the three most important things that you want in life. On a sheet of paper with your three most important goals, set down two of the best ways to reach each goal.
2. Define the parameters of a lesson or task that you plan to accomplish by next week or next month. Think through every minute detail of what you will have to do to complete the lesson or task that you have set for yourself. Then let your hidden powers work.
3. Try to recall the names of ten people or places you cannot remember immediately. Then, record the number that come back to you at the end of 10, 20, 30, and 60 minutes.
4. Pray or wish, if you prefer, with all of your heart, strength, and determination for success in reaching a worthwhile goal. Plan and work to make your wish come true. At the end of sufficient time, see how close you have come to your goal. Why did you get that far? If you did not reach a particular part of your goal, why not?
5. In a field of your choice, make a list of the great men and women of all time who have utilized their hidden powers for enviable success.

CHAPTER TWO

How to Succeed Through Willpower

You actually *will* your success, or you will your failure. Psychologists agree that each person has the power to choose his or her degree of success within the range of personal capabilities. If you want to succeed above all else, you will generate enough willpower to carry you through. The Declaration of Independence and the Constitution guaranteed freedom of choice. You are free to exert your own willpower. Exert it positively. Exert willpower for success.

Why Succeed?

We all arrive on this planet with a limited number of years, months, days, hours, and minutes. During these precious few moments, we have freedom of choice: We have the freedom to succeed or to fail.

Success brings security, satisfaction, and happiness. Failure brings frustration, hardship, and unhappiness. There are no happy failures. Success wears many faces. Children experience success on their report cards and on the sand lot. Adults earn the love and respect of others, build better bodies, pray for right and justice, become better people, earn money, paint pictures, or excel in music or martial arts, and achieve personal adjustment. Happy is the man or woman who uses willpower to succeed socially, economically, academically, artistically, spiritually, and personally. The good life is a successful life.

Success and Self-Image

Teachers and counselors are well aware that each child builds a self-image or self-concept. Each child looks within and pictures a succeeding or failing self. While the tendency is to see the self as static, in reality the image we have of ourselves is not even close to what really is the case. The growth of this self-image can be redirected and accelerated by the individual. Individuals build their own self-confidence and self-esteem. George Bernard Shaw said, "Success covers a multitude of blunders."

Self-image is like a tree. It grows from both internal and external influences. If a tree is scrawny and stunted, water and sunlight will not produce the same kind of growth that it does from a healthy, robust sapling. Just so, the self-image for success will grow faster in some individuals than in others with the same external stimulation. For success, the individual must choose external stimulation that nurtures a positive self-image.

What Do We Mean by Will and Willpower?

Modern psychologists have tended to tiptoe around the fact of the human will and have retreated without giving it full recognition and definition. Several schools of thought in psychology have looked the other way when confronted with such an intangible as the "will," which is just as intangible as the human "mind." But the will and the mind are there and will not go away.

Modern psychologists are not alone in treating the human will as a fuzzy concept. Plato and Aristotle confused the will with "reason." They misconstrued willpower as "representing the purpose of nature," which in Greek philosophy meant a semblance of the ideal. Then came the Christian doctrine, linking will to sin, dissipation, and disobedience to God. To be willful was to defy the Lord of the universe. St. Augustine lifted willpower a short way from its negative aspect. He maintained that man could use his will to attain grace by choosing the ways of God.

Philosophers such as Kant, Descartes, and Hume fell into the trap of looking on will as merely the opposite of determinism or predestination. In a more modern settling, Pavlov's classic experiment with dogs tended to set the will aside in favor of "conditioning," or automatic reacting to a repeated stimulation-and-reward sequence. The apostles of Pavlov overlooked the fact that human beings have a far greater capacity for choice and decision-making than do members of the canine species.

Freud, with his emphasis on unconscious forces in motivation, tended to look on will as a result of what was happening deep in the unconscious mind. He slighted the role played by conscious control and direction of the will. J.B. Watson, the noted father of behaviorism, tried to solve the problem of self-directed willpower by ignoring it just as he tried to ignore the mind. Since Watson could not find the mind or the will in a test-tube, he gave little significance to will as such. In viewing willpower as a means, Watson stressed activity — behavior itself — as an end product. To the behaviorist, it if couldn't be weighed or measured, it was without meaning and unworthy of study.

Actually, the importance of the will and willpower as means to success has found support among modern business and organizational psychologists. These practitioners, as opposed to theoreticians, have found that the human will can be strengthened, guided, and sustained. They have been quick to recognize that success in the business world depends upon the individual's indomitable and persistent will to bring it about. B.F. Skinner agreed with this modern concept: will as an urge toward a defined goal.

Will or willpower then, as used in this text, can be thought of as an inner urge, nourished by outward guiding forces toward the attainment of a significant goal — the goal of success. The will is a power plant with a range of capacity. It can be fed by individual desires and purposes that propel the individual toward success. When the will is strong and positive, the chances of attainment and success are good. When an indomitable will is riding on the back of high capability, success is assured.

A Measure of Willpower

Willpower is a human characteristic. When compared in large group of people, all human characteristics fall on a normal probability curve, sometimes called a bell-shaped curve. Statisticians point out that measured characteristics, such as the willpower of each individual in a large group of individuals selected at random, can be expressed by the normal probability curve. Few of us have very low willpower, and few have very high willpower. About 50% of the population ranks near the average (the middle of the curve) in strength of willpower.

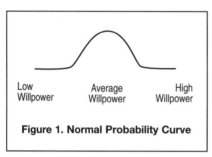

Low Willpower   Average Willpower   High Willpower

Figure 1. Normal Probability Curve

With this figure in mind, you can pick out individuals among your acquaintances who rank high or low in the characteristic of willpower. Most of the people you know will rank close enough to the average so that you cannot observe marked differences.

The important thing to remember about your own willpower is that it is not static. It can be changed. It can be strengthened. Wherever your willpower rating slides down on the low willpower end of the bell-shaped curve, with conscious effort you can move it toward the high willpower end. Your willpower is the result of a complicated composite of internal and external forces, but it mostly certainly is not preordained. You are the captain of your soul and the master of your own willpower. Change it! General Douglas MacArthur said, "There is no security on this earth; there is only opportunity."

How to Strengthen Your Willpower

Yes, your willpower is a complicated composite. Call forth your hidden powers to strengthen your will. You may not be able to recognize and strengthen all of the elements that influence your willpower, but you can change some of them — and some will be sufficient for success.

Try a few techniques that will move your willpower measurement from low to high on the bell-shaped curve:

1. *Choose a Goal.* You may choose several goals to work on, but do not choose too many goals to start. Do you want to play a musical instrument, make $100,000 a year, or become a better father or mother? If you are a student, how about getting all A's and B's? Or a part in a school play? Choose and focus on the goal or goals. Dostoevsky says, "Without some goal and some effort to reach it, no man can live."

2. *Set Daily (or Short-Term) Objectives.* A goal is like a finish line. Getting to the finish line may take time, but each day you can move closer. Daily objectives move you in the right direction. If your goal is to learn a foreign language, you can set a daily objective, for example, "to pronounce correctly 20 proper names." Tomorrow your objective might be "learning 20 new vocabulary words and their translation." For the next day, you can set as an objective, "to memorize how to conjugate a list of common verbs." Each daily objective will carry you closer to your goal.

3. *Focus Your Energies.* If your goal is to make more money next year, concentrate your energies and direct them toward money-making. Suppose you work as a life insurance agent. You cannot take time to study petroglyphs in the high Andes. You must stay home and focus your energies on sales. You must set a daily objective, for example, to develop a firm schedule for visiting customers. You'll miss some shows, and books will lie unread. You may not achieve a goal of making a million dollars, but you certainly can "make more money next year" (a realistic goal) if you focus your energies and exert willpower to keep them focused.

4. *Choose Successful Techniques.* Mark Twain's famous characters, Tom Sawyer and Huckleberry Finn, chose a bent spoon to dig a tunnel under an imagined prison wall. Tom had read too many escape stories. After a few blisters and minimal earth displacement, Tom figured they could use a spade and just pretend it was a bent spoon. With a chosen goal, defined objectives, and focused energy in place, next choose techniques and strategies that will advance you steadily toward your goal. For example, one brash real-estate agent finished his training and immediately set out to

sell multimillion-dollar industrial buildings. Another young agent chose the strategy of selling small residences, vacant lots, anything that small investors would buy. This agent set short-term, realistic — achievable — objectives. His business grew and grew in volume. He reached his goals and truly was a success. The salesman with the multimillion-dollar goal never did achieve success in real estate. He eventually left the field and took a job as a salesperson in a discount store. Choose successful techniques that will take you day by day toward your chosen goal.

5. *Learn to Enjoy Your Work.* You can control your state of mind. Unfortunately, too many people do control their minds in the wrong way. They grouse, grumble, fuss and complain. They look on the negative as being smart, sophisticated, the "in" thing to do. Avoid that trap because it will stop you on your way to success. Harry Truman enjoyed telling a story of the negative and positive boys. The negative boy was given every imaginable new toy at Christmas and left alone in his room for 30 minutes. At the end of the time he was scowling and angry because a wind-up key was lost and he had cut his fingers on a toy tank. The positive boy was given a pile of horse manure with a toy shovel that had a broken handle. But when they looked in on him at the end of 30 minutes, his besmirched face was full of smiles and he said, "With all this 'stuff' around, there must be a horse down there somewhere!"

Be happy at your work. Don't postpone all of your enjoyment until the job is complete. You spend a large percentage of your waking hours thinking about, planning for, and doing your job. So if you are not happy at your work, you are bound to Shakespeare's "shallows and miseries." A prominent woman who is the editor of a leading fashion magazine said, "My deepest and most enduring satisfactions occur between 9 a.m. and 5 p.m." Yes, you control your state of mind. Learn to enjoy your work. Reward yourself with the satisfaction of success. Smile! Put your sunny side up. A smile on your face can reach deep into your subconscious mind and work wonders. There must be a horse down there somewhere!

6. *Practice.* "Practice makes perfect," so they say. But if practice never quite achieves perfection, it does move you closer to your chosen goal. Whether you practice kicking field goals, sewing in a zipper, performing a martial arts technique, playing Hamlet, tracking pulsars, or skinning a fish, your repeated experiences lead toward your goal. If you have a speech to give, practice before the mirror. If possible, practice it in the same place where you will give it. You must make that place your own — your home field. Practice in front of a critical friend. Shoot baskets or kick goals for hours if you want to make the team. Set up an audience of stuffed animals or dolls if you're going to teach a kindergarten class, or preach a sermon to stumps in a forest. Demosthenes spoke to the pounding surf with a mouth full of stones and became the

TIPS FOR SUCCESS

- Set realistic goals.
- Develop daily, or short-term, objectives that move you toward your goals.
- Activate your desire to succeed.
- Focus on your goals and how to achieve them.
- Use mental imagery to "see" exactly what you want to accomplish.

greatest orator in Athens. Practice is one of the best tests of your willpower. It is much easier to take a music lesson than it is later to practice that lesson for hours. It is said that the great Paderewski was never completely satisfied with a performance. He would go back and practice and practice and then he would practice some more. Over-learning, or continuing to practice after we can do something correctly, results in improved performance. With over-learning, you will do whatever it is even better. Over-learning works! Develop the willpower that leads you to practice, practice, and more practice. Then, Eureka! Success.

7. *Don't Give Up.* Sometimes when we think we know all there is to know about some topic, or we don't seem to be making progress, we have reached a plateau. Boredom sets in. Or we are no longer motivated because we are discouraged. We do not think

we are going to go beyond our plateau. A football team hopeful at USC was dejected. He had failed to complete his first ten practice test kicks successfully. He looked the picture of failure as he sat on the bench awaiting the verdict of the coaches. Then he made a crucial decision: He decided to spend as much time as it took for him to reach his objectives. He spent hours practicing long after the rest of the team had left the field for the day. Finally, when the time came for his third trial test, he scored 100 points more than he needed. He reached his goal — and so did USC.

A 60-six year old woman with multiple sclerosis decided she needed to relax, to fight her disease and be able to move better, and at the same time to be able to defend herself. She enrolled in a jujitsu/kenpo/kung fu course at the Burbank YMCA, and a mushin ryu ju jitsu self-defense class at the Torrance YMCA. She volunteered to teach self-defense to children. Through diligent practice, practice, and more practice, she earned promotions through the ranks until today she holds a black belt.

Neither the football kicker nor the black belt senior ever gave up. Hang in there for success. Never surrender!

8. *Measure Your Progress.* If you achieve your daily objectives and move a little closer to your chosen goal, you should know it. Knowledge of your progress will serve as a reward for your accomplishment. Your achievements (and what you have learned) would be "reinforced," as B.F. Skinner and Edwin Thorndike put it. Any self-made record of your progress will do. Usually, you can keep a simple chart. Add each day's progress. An uncomplicated line graph would do; the simpler the better. It may sound silly, but it works. Maybe your goal is to weigh what you weighed in high school. Then keep a weight chart near the bathroom scale. If you want to quit smoking, count the fewer cigarettes each day. If you are a salesman, count the number of sales or the volume of business. And remember to reward yourself. You'll deserve it.

If you wish to measure your progress in a more complicated activity, such as growing corn, check the results of your yearly selection of hybrid seed, time of planting, fertilization, cultivation, water supply if using irrigation, and methods of harvesting. If you teach a history class, check your planning, motivational devices, materials of instruction, student participation, observed interest in the lesson, and results on objective tests. Measure your progress as a teacher again on tomorrow's lesson. Whatever you do — from hopscotch to brain surgery — measure your progress. See your success in tangible form — and be happy!

9. *Revise Your Techniques and Press On.* As you measure and evaluate your progress toward your chosen goal, and continue to practice, you will find techniques that could be more effective. Psychological research shows that you will move faster and faster the closer you come to your goal. Suppose you are a salesman. Is your prospecting effective? Do you establish rapport with clients? Do you tell them what they want to know or what you want them to know? Do you close the contract in the way that gives them what they need?

As you examine your techniques, have they not only been effective, but *most* effective?

In the story, "Acres of Diamonds," stress was laid on the wants and needs of the buyer, the buyer who needed a specific kind of pocketknife. Have you served the customer, or have you thought too much about your own profits? Your own profits will be greater when you serve the customer to the best of your ability. Revise your methods, techniques, and strategies following measurement and evaluation. Be sure your strategies for goal attainment are most effective. Then press on. Mobilize your total willpower toward success.

Taking Stock of Your Willpower

When you have used some of these techniques to strengthen your own willpower, try to rank yourself on the normal curve. Observe your acquaintances and compare yourself with them. Think of fictional and historic characters, and compare your willpower with theirs. When you review the biographies of highly successful people, you will find amazing correlation between an individual's achievement and his or her determination.

One example of a person with strong willpower comes quickly to mind, Winston Churchill. Mr. Churchill was defeated in South Africa and at Gallipoli, but he came back stronger. He lost his seat in Parliament only to return with greater power. He opposed Hitler when those about him cowered and appeased. When crisis came to Western Europe, Churchill never quavered. Nation after nation surrendered, but he had the willpower to resist the horrifying bombs even after losing Dunkirk. His goal was to win the war, and he would do so even if he had to lose many of the battles.

It was said that Churchill mobilized the English language and took it to war. This is just half of the story. In his "Finest Hour" and "Blood, Sweat, and Tears" speeches, he was using language to strengthen his own will to resist and to strengthen the willpower of a physically beaten people. Like a ball thrown against a wall, Churchill bounced back. With strong willpower, you too can bounce back — and bounce to success.

Churchill demonstrated clearly that victory need not go to the strong of arm, but to the strong of will. When the will to win is there, a way will be found. Churchill found the way, waiting for the arsenal of America to be zeroed in on the Nazi hordes over-running Europe, the Near East, and Northern Africa.

The willpower of Churchill was enough to inspire other great leaders, including Franklin D. Roosevelt and Dwight D. Eisenhower. Walter Lippman wrote in 1943, "The final test of a leader is that he leaves behind him in other men the conviction and the will to carry on." Great leaders did carry on until victory was complete and success assured.

Few of us will ever have the terrible responsibility or the golden opportunity that came to Winston Churchill. But every day there are situations that call in some small way for willpower from each of us. If you shake off apathy and choose a worthwhile goal, then the driving force of willpower can lead you to success.

President John F. Kennedy set the goal of putting an American on the moon before the end of the decade. Before the 1960s ended, through national resolve — willpower — that goal was reached. Remember: To succeed you must have the *will* to succeed. Success leads to satisfaction and happiness. A positive self-image strengthens willpower, the kind of willpower that drives you toward a chosen goal. This willpower differs among people and can be represented by a bell-shaped curve. Your place on the curve can be improved by such strategies as goal-orientation, focus, and conservation of energy; work satisfaction, practice, redirection, and improved techniques. The great achievers of all ages have had strong willpower. You, too, can enjoy success by force of will. Bear in mind the words of Benjamin Disraeli, the great British prime minister of the Victorian era, who said, "The secret of success is constancy of purpose."

Things to Do

This chapter has been about willpower, what it is and how to strengthen it. Following are some activities that will hone the concepts.

1. To strengthen your own willpower, each day work on some worthwhile task that you previously disliked.
2. Draw a bell-shaped curve and place a mark somewhere between "low willpower" and "high willpower" to represent the strength of your willpower. Then consider how to move that mark in the "high willpower" direction.
3. On a sheet of paper, write down at least three long-term goals. Put at least two short-term objectives under each goal.
4. List six people, real or fictional, who you would say are characterized by strong willpower.

CHAPTER THREE

How to Improve Your Capacity for Success

The *U.S. Dictionary of Occupational Titles* lists thousands of ways to make a living in any metropolitan area. Each person has success capabilities, not only in occupations, but in broader endeavors: in human relations, athletics, the arts, science, invention, exploration, and many others. One of the greatest qualities for success is the ability to build and improve in the area of human relations.

Do you want to be rich? You can. Do you want to be a forceful speaker? Do you want to win public office? You can! Success is outstanding accomplishment. Some degree of accomplishment is always possible. When used to their maximum, capacity and willpower open the magic doors of success.

The range of capacities in any normal human being is so great that most of the individual's capabilities never get discovered. During thousands of years, mankind has had the capability of building an automobile, inventing the telephone, flying through the air, and rocketing to the moon. But those capacities lay buried and dormant until unique environmental circumstances called them forth.

In a vague way, people have always been conscious of their great range of abilities. Confucius spoke of the many faces of man. The Greeks created myths, which told of the physical strength of Hercules and the beauty of Aphrodite. The Bible refers to men of varied talents. Your own talents are so varied and your hidden abilities so limitless that you really can achieve your wildest dreams. Your set of capabilities is like a rocket engine. When fired by the drive of willpower, you can orbit into your chosen realm of success.

Are We All Born Equal?

Of the more than six billion people who have lived on the earth, no one before has ever looked just like you or had your inherent capabilities for success. You are unique. You can be successful in a way that no other human being can. You have a different combination of capacities, possessed by you and you alone. Your task is to find your unique excellence and press willpower full throttle toward your chosen goal.

When our founding fathers wrote, "all men are created equal," they were not referring to the capacity for success. They meant equality under the law. Boys and girls, men and women are born unequal in abilities, and the inequalities become greater throughout life. No one in his right mind could argue effectively that all people have equal capacity in every trait, but all fair-minded people can argue that people should have equal opportunity.

In modern America, we enjoy the greatest freedom of choice ever known. We are not slaves, serfs, or servants of class. We are free to choose goal-oriented success based on our interests, capacities, and strength of will. You can actually plan and choose your own degree of success.

Know Your Inherited Capacities

Intelligence quotients, performance tests, interest inventories, sociograms, composite profiles, DNA, and genes are relatively new developments or discoveries. In past ages, physical capacity and artistic ability have been more measurable than reasoning, judgment, memory, human relations, personal adjustment, and spiritual fulfillment.

Physical endurance has been more measurable since Pheidippides raced more than 20 miles from the Battle of Marathon to gasp out news of victory in the Agora, the Athens marketplace.

Intelligence testing as pioneered by Binet, Terman, Wechsler, and others, along with attitude and interest inventories, are products of the 20th century. DNA and genes are latecomers to concepts of capacity and character.

Whether capacities for success can be measured, or measured with great accuracy, is beside the point. We know that they exist, and we know that they differ in every individual. You know that you have the capacity to succeed to some degree in an almost limitless list of endeavors. You also know that you can excel by combining those unique capacities. Psychologist William James calls these capacities "inherited reservoirs of ability" — your hidden powers.

When you compare yourself with others in a large group, you know that your capacity for long-distance jogging, playing the piano, explaining the latest developments in computer technology, playing chess, performing mental calculations, or learning the list of spelling demons, will fall somewhere on the normal curve. You also know that your standing can be improved.

If we could get true measures of our individual capacities and compare them with others on the normal probability curve, we would have a better basis for choosing goals for success. This is what career counseling is supposed to be about. Both youths and adults may get help in discovering their individual interests and capabilities. The interests and abilities should be matched with opportunities — in jobs, sports, aesthetics, government, religion, education, communications, discovery, and personal affairs. Wise choices based on unique capacities and in line with existing opportunities need only willpower to ensure success.

Determiners of Success

Physiologically and psychologically innate capabilities dwell within the human body. Success in almost any endeavor demands a whole body; a body that stands with great reservoirs of hidden power. But it can be easy to get sidetracked. A quarterback for the Dallas Cowboys had trouble throwing forward passes when he had a sore heel. A college student failed Chemistry IV when his mother-in-law came to visit his wife and him in what he saw as their "cramped" apartment.

Even though most accomplishments depend on total-person reactions, some parts of the body play a chief role in human accomplishment. The brain and the hand, with its opposable thumb, is what sets us apart from all other animal species. Psychologically, the brain makes possible the choosing of goals, planning adequate techniques for their attainment, and developing the driving force of willpower to persist and stay on course. As far as we know, the lower animals are incapable of consciously choosing and setting goals for themselves. They exist in the present without the capacity of projecting themselves into the future. While they do have built-in instincts, they lack planning direction and the choice of strategies needed to achieve long-range goals. Thousands of generations of grasshoppers have never been able to avoid freezing in November.

TIPS FOR SUCCESS

- See the potential in others and notice how they have improved on their inherited capacities.

- Assess your own capabilities. Jot them down and earmark those to improve.

- Realize that no one is "jinxed" or "just lucky." Make your own luck.

The human hand is the instrument that carries out the plans originating in the brain. Physiologically and neurologically, the brain and hand are a billion miracles that statistically could not have happened, but did. Even though the brain weighs little more than three pounds, it is made of billions of interconnecting cells with trillions of connections, or "synapses." This masterpiece of communication makes the most complicated nerve center of the telephone system look as crude as Gutenberg's jumble of movable type appears to today's computer users.

With this kind of human "equipment," nothing can hold you back. But if your capacities are sleeping, you cannot achieve success. Wake them up!

You Can Improve Your Inherited Capacities

Inherited capacity is an undetermined reservoir of potential. You can let the reservoir shrink and dry up, or you can fill it to overflowing. The old idea of being limited to your inheritance is nonsense. Almost everyone can learn to bake cookies or play the flute to some degree. The inherited capacity is there. Yet how many flute players are running loose in our streets? We may be threatened with a plague of grasshoppers or con men, but not with flute players. Few people ever arouse their myriad of sleeping capacities.

Overcome Challenges. Helen Keller had all the strikes against her. To grow up blind and deaf was to be at the bottom of the normal curve in inherited capacity. But in spite of, and to some degree because of, her handicap she became internationally famous. Thomas A. Edison had impaired hearing, and so he spent endless hours working on his inventions in his laboratory. Theodore "Teddy" Roosevelt was a sickly youth, and so he became leader of the "Rough Riders." These individuals overcame inherited challenges by force of will.

Consider another example. Mary Hudson was a young girl in Kansas City who knew nothing about the oil business or service stations. But she refused to "know her place" and concede that running a service station was a "man's job." Instead, Mary borrowed $200 from her father as down payment on a service station and tapped her capacity to become a success. Because she had the handicap of being a female in the service station business, she worked harder. By the age of 30, Mary Hudson was a millionaire. She was listed recently by *Fortune* magazine as one of America's richest persons, those who had a net worth of fifty million dollars or more.

Mary Hudson struggled to survive and then succeed during the Great Depression. If she could overcome the capacity handicap of being a woman in what was considered a man's job, what is holding you back? Choose your career. You do have the capabilities. Do not keep success waiting any longer. Genius is often the result of overcoming the challenge of a perceived handicap. You are not limited by your inheritance. Take what you have and make your own success.

Blaming your family tree is the surest way to beat yourself out of the success you deserve. No, your grandfather did not cheat you. Doubting your capacity is cheating yourself. While you are doubting your capacity, you are drying up the amount of capability that you do have.

Maintain and Strengthen Your Capacities. Even in biblical days, it was known that capacity could be increased or decreased. "For unto every one that hath shall be given, and he shall have abundance: but from him that hath not shall be taken away even that which he hath" (Matthew 25:29). Use your capacity for success, and you will have more. Tie your right arm in a sling, and your muscles of success will atrophy.

Benjamin Franklin is an example of someone who improved his capacity. Franklin was born of relatively undistinguished middle-class parentage. He was unable to pay for education at Harvard, so he set out to be his own teacher and to improve his ability in many ways. He landed in Philadelphia in 1723, with one Dutch dollar in his pocket. Young Benjamin had little time to explore his many capacities and choose the strongest. He was apprenticed to his older brother, James, and thrust into the printing trade. But while setting type, Benjamin sought out models of English writing and practiced writing as well or better. He taught himself to be an orator, to debate, to converse.

Benjamin Franklin was not satisfied to let his capacities sleep or dry up. He organized a group of intellectuals called the "Junta" to explore any and all avenues of social, financial, scientific, or political success. With driving willpower and the fine honing of his diverse capacities, he became financially independent at 42 and chose to devote the remainder of his long life to science and public service.

To keep his own capacities growing and to help others, Benjamin Franklin started a circulating library and founded the American Philosophical Society. He experimented with electricity; suggested the founding of an academy in Philadelphia (which later became the University of Pennsylvania), and wrote *Poor Richard's Almanac*. He invented the cook stove, bifocals, and the lightning rod. He ran for public office and advocated colonial expansion to the West.

Few Canadians appreciate how much their future was affected by Benjamin Franklin. As Agent of Pennsylvania in London, Franklin used his influence toward conclusion of the Seven Years' War (1756-1763) with France. At the end of the war, England could acquire Canada or the rich sugar-producing Guadeloupe in the West Indies. Franklin threw his persuasive social, conversational, and diplomatic power behind the choice of Canada. English parliamentarians listened to Franklin's eloquent descriptions of that endless, unexplored "empire" stretching from the Atlantic to the Pacific, and chose Canada.

Most Americans are familiar with the way Franklin used his many capacities to advance the cause of the colonies on both sides of the Atlantic. What they need to recognize is that Benjamin Franklin accepted the raw material of an unknown colonial boy's talents and, by conscious improvement, built many superior capacities.

He believed what Thomas A. Edison later said: "Genius is one percent inspiration and ninety-nine percent perspiration."

No Exceptions

Benjamin Franklin is not a rare exception. Books of history and biography are filled with instances where men and women of given, sometimes limited, capacities have attained great successes because they improved their inherited capacities.

Psychologists know that what people think of as one's inherited capacities can be improved. They are not sure how much. What is the limit? Is there a limit? Records in athletics, industry, agriculture, commerce, and all other measurable activities are being broken. Then the new records will be broken, too.

Because all people have many capacities and because all capacities can be improved, how much are you willing to exert your willpower toward improvement? Improved abilities turn that fleeting dream of success to reality.

Your psychological and physical hidden powers for success lie mostly in your brain. I once wrote that a telephone system to match the interconnections of your brain would have to be as big as Kansas. A television program titled "Understanding the Brain" reported that the brain has 1,000 trillion connections. This is your unfathomable hidden power for success.

Things to Do

In this chapter, we have focused on capacity for success, discovering them and improving them. Following are some activities that may help you realize and strengthen your capabilities.

1. Which is more important in achieving success, heredity or environment? List arguments for each.
2. Note, in order of importance, five of your unique capabilities. In what areas will each of your strengths lead you to success?
3. If the brain and the hand make human beings masters of all life, can you think of special ways that these organs can contribute to greater success for you?
4. Records in athletics, technology, economics, and other areas continue to fall. With your capacity and drive, is there a record that you can challenge?

CHAPTER FOUR

How to Succeed Through Lifelong Learning

If you wish to be successful, you must learn, learn, learn, and keep on learning. In former times, students graduated from the eighth grade, from high school, or from college and felt educated for life in a slowly changing world. Now the winds of change blow so fast that yesterday's learning is out of date before we reach tomorrow. The average person will now change occupations four or five times over a working life. Vernon Law says, "When you're through learning, you're through."

The successful person in any field must spend a good portion of every year retraining to keep up with fast-breaking developments. Technology is expanding explosively. For example, a recent issue of *U.S. News & World Report* showed that the use of chemicals in the United States had expanded from a few hundred in 1940 to more than 70,000 by the end of the century. Changes in all other areas are similar: They all show positive acceleration. Students in schools of medicine, engineering, and commerce, as well as practicing physicians, electronic technicians, businessmen, teachers, and auto mechanics all have the daunting task of attempting to keep pace with such change.

Preservice and Inservice Education

If you desire success, your lifelong learning will consist of preservice and inservice education, multiple times if you change careers. Preservice education is both general and specialized. Inservice education is more often specialized and both theoretical and practical. From cradle to grave, you *must* be learning. Learning is requisite for success. A maxim to live by is this: Success must be learned and earned.

Preservice Education. Child labor laws and other restrictions prohibit children from much real participation in the world of work. Childhood, however, is the first period of preservice education. Once upon a time, children had no formal education until they entered first grade at about six years of age. But today there is greater emphasis on early childhood and "pre-school" education beginning at a very early age in the home and continuing in private or public schools. Kindergarten has become a standard experience throughout the country.

During the elementary school years, emphasis is placed on learning the fundamental processes of reading, writing, calculation, and some understanding of the social, cultural, historical, scientific, and artistic characteristics of our age. This type of education is general and is needed by all.

During middle and high school and in later studies, students continue general education in the humanities, in scientific and in artistic fields, and gradually begin to specialize in areas chosen to lead toward a successful career. Through all grades and phases of preservice education, the three most valuable learned competencies are: a high degree of facility in the English language, skill in basic mathematics, and mastery of harmonious human relations.

Other areas of concentration are career-, accomplishment-, and goal-oriented. During their preservice education, students may specialize in such areas as agriculture, mining, music and art, science and engineering, government and law, healing, sales, communication, foreign language, education, and many others. These specializations represent an attempt to keep pace with a runaway list of new and existing occupations.

Mark Twain once said humorously, "Training is everything. The peach was once a bitter almond; cauliflower is but cabbage with a college education."

Inservice Education. Regardless of whether you trained for teaching, merchandising, transportation, or farming, the constant demand for new learning will continue after your entry into any given field. When what you desire is the highest degree of success in a field, you must seize every opportunity for personal and professional growth. Lifelong learning will help you to become and remain successful.

Inservice education can be difficult because it often amounts to self-education. As a student in preservice education, from kindergarten through the 12th grade or even through the community college and higher, you were directed by parents, teachers, and counselors. Suddenly, there are no imposed lessons. You are left without direction. You are on your own. It's easy to become bewildered and unsure. This is a real test of your character. This is the time that you choose your degree of success.

> ## SPECIAL ADVICE TO STUDENTS
>
> If you are a student, you need to know about the vast array of specialized training and careers open to you. Seek information from parents, teachers, counselors, and people working in the area you are considering. Try to match your capabilities and interests with the job opportunities available. Then test your choices by actually doing some of the work involved in a given field.
>
> Caution: Be aware that specialized training will not prepare you *permanently* for the demands of any career. You will have the education needed to enter your chosen career, but it will take a commitment to ongoing — lifelong — learning to make you truly successful in that career.

So don't waste your time. Don't put off further training until next year. Don't wait for someone to coax you into an inservice class. But neither should you jump at just any type of training, perhaps because your best friend is taking it. Take time to make yourself a long-term plan. Plan this program as carefully as if your life depended on it. Actually, your occupational life does depend upon it. As you plan, you are determining your degree of success in life. It is up to you. Do you have the initiative to overcome the pitfalls of procrastination, seeking easy shortcuts, or wallowing in indecision?

Commonsense Inservice Education

Your best inservice education opportunity is your job itself. Learn to do that job better every day that you go to work. Don't be satisfied with mediocre performance and with being a clock-watcher. Giving anything less than the best to your job cheats you out of your chances for greater success. Not only should you increase the quality of your performance, but you also should seek new experiences in the same job situation. If you work in a retail store, learn every phase of the total business. Learn the intricacies of the local computer operations, learn to sell, to display, to keep the inventories, to order, to warehouse, to advertise, to tend to the accounts, to clean up the place, to introduce new employees to their duties, and, above all, to improve relations with customers.

In addition to improving your job efficiency, you may wish to train for advancement. You can train for advancement in your own job or in another career. Training for greater proficiency in your own job often is the best means of gaining entry into a more desirable career.

> **TIPS FOR SUCCESS**
>
> • Know where you are, what you can do, and what you need to learn through continuous self-evaluation.
>
> • Be flexible: ready to change and capable of change.
>
> • Take action to gain the skills and knowledge you need to succeed.
>
> • Stay involved, and work for self-improvement.
>
> • Ask for advice, and then make informed decisions about career advancement or change.
>
> • Don't let temporary setbacks become permanent impediments to success.

Be Prepared for the Knock of Opportunity

While you are working on the job, you should plan for greater and greater successes. Your greater success will be possible only if you have added to or increased your skills and made yourself more proficient *before* opportunity knocks. To illustrate, suppose you are a stenographer with a typing speed of 60 words per minute, but you take no more training to increase your speed. Then a position opens up paying a much higher salary but requiring a speed of 70 words per minute. If you have not already increased your speed, the new position is no opportunity for you. In fact, you cannot even apply for the position.

It is said that opportunity knocks only at the door of those who are prepared. It has also been said that real "luck" is 95% preparation and only 5% chance.

Another word of advice: Be alert to potential opportunities in entirely new fields of endeavor. Remember, there was a time when *nobody* was a computer programmer or technician.

Many opportunities exist, but the training of the applicant must match requirements in the job specifications. To further train yourself, you may be able to take a leave of absence from your job and study full time. A community college or a university may be available nearby. Relatively few people can afford to take such leaves, but you may be one of the lucky ones. Most of us, however, must seek additional training while on the job. Nevertheless, remember what E. A. Filene said, "If a man's education is finished, he is finished."

You can continue on the job and still pursue your lifelong learning program by enrolling in evening adult classes in high schools, weekend or evening sessions at community colleges, through courses of instruction offered at private and technical schools, and through participation in correspondence courses. You can pursue self-directed library research and even seek out evening apprenticeship work in other fields. There are opportunities for observing others at work in their careers. Some educational television channels offer broadcast courses at the college level. In all cases, the choice is yours. Also in all cases, the responsibility for obtaining greater training rests squarely on you and you alone. Some companies offer rewards, such as release time or tuition reimbursement, for those who pursue inservice education. If such a program fits your needs, by all means grasp the opportunity.

A Word of Caution

Remember that your goal is lifelong learning. Do not try to get all of your learning in a week, a month, or a year. You have to live and to be a well-rounded human being, and so you need some time for leisure and diversion. You have family obligations, which should not be ignored. Plan for the long-term. Don't fall into the "get-rich-quick learning and it's over" trap.

Avoid the mistake of Mr. Bright Boy who bragged in college that he would be a millionaire and retire before he was 35. His plan worked, but he became a miserable human being in retirement partly because "there were no more worlds to conquer." Your greatest satisfactions in learning will come with continuing growth — with the kind of continuing growth that will enrich the second half of a productive life as well as the first. The extremes of trying to learn everything all at once or postponing it indefinitely are equally wrong. Somewhere in between is the golden mean of satisfying success.

The Choice Is Yours

It is tough to plan studies that cut out long evenings gabbing with friends or sitting before the television, weekends at games, and sociable lounging during the coffee breaks. Make better use of your time. But remember that 50% of your co-workers will always do less than an average (mediocre) job. Only a small percentage of your colleagues will rise to the top. You should be one of them. The choice is up to you. Yes, it is tough to deny yourself temporary enjoyments, but when the going is tough, the tough get going. Isn't that the saying? So get going.

I was principal of the University Evening Adult School in Los Angeles when Bill Spalding came to enroll in Spanish. Bill was a successful head football coach and was nearing retirement. This was just one more step in Spalding's long learning career. When asked why he was studying Spanish, he said that facility in the language would help in talking with the families of Hispanic football players and would help him to communicate more effectively in general. And it would be a source of personal satisfaction when he traveled in Mexico.

Grandma Moses was still learning in her 80s and claimed that her greatest satisfactions in living came after the time when many people wither on the vine. I can point with some pride to myself, having published a new book, *The Homesteaders*, at age 96. As of this writing, incidentally, I am 99 and still tremendously successful in my second career in estate planning, helping people make millions — a career I did not begin until age 70.

Ralph Waldo Emerson is another example of a lifetime scholar. Through his long life, he felt the day wasted if he went to bed without learning something new. His lectures and essays were crammed with new concepts and ways of expressing "eternal truths" in a different and exciting style.

Psychologists recognize that youth assemble enough facts, concepts, and skills to enter a career. Through a program of lifelong learning, they can advance to great successes through one or a succession of careers. Then, if they choose, they can retire. But true lifelong learners never really retire; they simply change focus. My maxim: Never retire! Keep improving your successes, and make a tiny bit of the world better.

Things to Do

The thrust of this chapter has been to point out the importance of lifelong learning. Following are some ideas so that you can take charge of your own learning.

1. Consider: What areas of general education are best for you? What specialized instruction do you need?
2. What career do you want to pursue, or what form of advancement or change do you desire?
3. List the minimum knowledge and skills that you need in order to obtain the position you desire.
4. List 10 ways to do your job better.
5. Plan a course of study, which will prepare you for a new position or advancement.

6. Consider ways to enhance self-discipline and increase enjoyment of your lifelong learning program.
7. Collect and study samples of job or assignment specifications that indicate required training.
8. Read biographies of highly successful individuals in your chosen field of work. How did they prepare for their careers?

CHAPTER FIVE

How to Develop
Habits of Success

Jean Jacques Rousseau advised people in the 18th century to form no habits at all lest spontaneity be stifled. He was a free-wheeling philosopher but a poor psychologist. The question is not *whether* you will form habits. You will. The question is whether your habits will lead to success or to failure.

Psychologists now tell us that habits are formed and grow in strength when acts are repeated. These acts may be mental, emotional, or physical. It is generally conceded that continuous repetition strengthens habits. Habits are built more rapidly when reinforced by having rewarding consequences and accompanying pleasant emotions.

It is important to remember that habits can be consciously formed. They can be planned with minute care. Playing the piano and typing involve carefully planned habit patterns. At the other extreme, unfavorable habits can be formed by neglect. A person can fall into careless habits. People can fall into the sloppy habits of unkempt dress, slurring their speech, or ignoring their friends. To use your habit system for the greatest success, you must carefully plan and improve your habits.

You have the right to choose your own habits. Seize this privilege and make your own success. You owe to yourself successful habits, your family deserves it, and your country expects it. Failure has no respectable place in the free-enterprise system.

It is impossible to list all of the habit patterns for the mental, emotional, social, occupational, and physical situations that you will confront. You will have to plan your own, but the following suggestions may help.

Think of Yourself as a Winner

The old saying goes, "A quitter never wins and a winner never quits." What you think you are, you will become. Establish and maintain thought patterns, which put you in the winner's circle. If you are a student, think of yourself as an A student. See yourself doing well, looking relaxed and confident. If you are an athlete, think of yourself — and, again, see yourself — as the best. If your job requires you to use a computer keyboard, think of yourself as having skill, speed, and accuracy. Get that image! Mental habits lead to physical fulfillment, and self-esteem is the doorway to success.

If you think of yourself — and have an image of yourself — as an A student, you are well on your way toward achieving that A. If it happens that you get a B or C, you have avoided a D or F. Think of your C or B as a steppingstone to the A. You are headed for the top of the mountain, and with winning mental habits, you will make it. Renew your commitment with that positive image.

Build the Habit of Enjoying Your Work

Instead of a Thank-God-It's-Friday attitude, build habits of Thank God-It's-Monday and a chance for more satisfying, fulfilling achievement. Your on-the job or in-class accomplishments can and should be exciting. The people of the world are not fed, healed, educated, served, or inspired while you are dawdling over the Sunday newspaper, playing video games, surfing the net, talking to friends on the telephone, or indulging in beer and potato chips.

Create habits of excitement about your job. There you are building a better world. Maybe your part is only routine, but you belong to a team that is helping people to be better fed, clothed, sheltered, educated, entertained, and to be healthier with greater mortality than any other generation since the beginning of time. Try feeling that your work is so important that you should be paying for the privilege of doing your job rather than vice versa.

When you build the habit of truly enjoying your work, you are laying the foundation for a happy life and for occupational success. Avoid habits that other employees have fallen into, such as dwelling on negatives or continuously grousing, grumbling, and complaining. Try focusing on the good things. There must be something good! Tell your supervisor and your fellow workers how much you appreciate the lighting system, the supplies that you work with, and your associates. Accentuate the positive and eliminate the negative, as the old song says. You'll be surprised how much better you will begin to like your job. Psychologically, it works. It works toward success.

Use the Golden Mean in Emotional Control

The Greeks called moderation in all things the "Golden Mean." They believed that extremes were vices and that moderately controlled behavior was a virtue.

For success in human relations, build habits of emotional control. Employees who fly off the handle and mouth off, blow their stack, or angrily tell off the boss are cheating no one but themselves. Try to follow the Greek maxim of moderation in your emotional reactions.

Psychologists recommend a delayed response. Whether you make a mental conclusion or an emotional reaction, it is better to make a considered, rather than a flighty, response. The axiom "count to ten" is good advice. Use it to cool off a hot head. And when a colleague at work or a fellow student throws an idea at you or elicits an emotional response, think. Take your time. Wait until all of the evidence is in. Consider it, and only then make your judgment. Abraham Lincoln agreed with this approach when he said, "It is better to remain silent and be thought a fool than to open your mouth and remove all doubt."

Follow Healthy Physical Habits

Good health habits make success possible. And the opposite also is true: Poor health habits make success unlikely. So much has been said about proper exercise, rest, avoiding the graveyard shift if at all possible, having a nutritionally sound diet, and avoiding stimulants or depressants and other substances, including tobacco, that only conclusions need to be stressed at this point.

If you wish to build habits that lead to success, start with health habits. Theodore Roosevelt inherited a frail body but built health habits that made him a robust man. His health habits made it possible for him to lead the "Rough Riders" up San Juan Hill and to be one of our most vigorous American presidents.

Whatever your health status may be, it can be improved. Your task is to select the habits that will help you most. These habits must provide you with a well-coordinated mind and body to carry you along the road to success.

Build the Habit of "Thinking Big"

A little-known teacher in Abilene, Kansas, told her mother at the end of a weary day, "My class is like an apple. I know how many seeds there are in the apple, but I don't know how many apples there are in each seed." Then she continued by saying, "There's Bruce, Debbie, Gary, Dwight, Diana, Glenn, Peter, Lori, ..." Years later this teacher went back and traced to see how many apples there had been in each seed that she nurtured in her classroom. Among those whose destiny she could little predict, she found that she had taught a YMCA secretary, a suicide, a mother of two sets of twins, a dairy farmer, a nurse, a state congressman, an emergency room doctor, and a country clerk and recorder. And then there was Dwight, who became a soldier, a campaigner in North Africa, Commander-in-Chief of Allied Forces in Europe, and President of the United States. Dwight David Eisenhower.

You don't know what heights you may attain. Build habits of reaching above and beyond your expected grasp. Look beyond the horizon and let your mind revel in limitless possibilities. Build habits of thinking big, the way they reputedly do in Texas. That kind of big thinking did not let Houston remain a muddy riverbank, but destined it to become a home of NASA, which would probe into interstellar spaces. You, too, must aim for the stars.

Little did David Dunbar Buick and William C. Durant dream on 28 December 1908 that by combining Buick and Oldsmobile they were forming one of the greatest industrial companies on earth, General Motors. That seed of imagination certainly bore fruit. It produced a worldwide orchard.

Habitually, set quotas for yourself. But think of these quotas as floors, not ceilings. Build habits of thinking big and surpassing. Think along with Reverend Robert Schuller, It's possible! Remember the Little Engine that Could, who huffed, "I think I can, I think I can," and you will find that it really is possible — it can be done.

TIPS FOR SUCCESS

- Accentuate the positive and eliminate the negative.

- Stop, think, count if you must, and only then react.

- Be an early bird — and tackle the hard tasks first.

- Say "no" to distractions.

- Never give up.

- See yourself as a success. Make the image work for you.

- Never stop learning.

Adopt the Habit of Being Early

That old adage that "the early bird gets the worm" is out of date. The early bird not only gets there in time for a good breakfast, but also gets to homestead the whole territory.

Whether you go out to plant corn, get a patent, or find oil, get there first. Start early. Build habits of being there not only on time, but before time. Waiting for the last possible moment to leave for that job interview or exam only invites disaster. If the least little thing goes wrong — a dead battery, a highway closed for maintenance, or a thousand other things — the result cannot be good.

If you are an administrative assistant, be in your seat with your morning snack completed, supplies ready, and work begun before the eight o'clock buzzer. If you build such habits of punctuality, reliability, and dependability, whom do you suppose will be named as office manager, you or Lillie Latecomer?

George Washington practiced habits of starting early. With his ragtag colonial army outnumbered four or five to one, he kept fooling the predictable British. Whether in crossing the Delaware or escaping from endangered campsites in the backcountry, he was always one jump ahead. His encirclement of Cornwallis at Yorktown was so early and so fast that the British, who still had sizable armed forces on the America continent, just called off the war on colonial terms. Washington *literally* deserved the compliment when he was proclaimed "first in war, first in peace, and first in the hearts of his countrymen."

Develop Effective Routines

If you are a student, establish a regular place to do your homework. Also establish a time schedule. Unless you reduce your homework to habit, you will waste important time before starting each assignment. Self-discipline puts you on the road to success. Develop an effective routine. Have all equipment and supplies at hand, and avoid distractions. Your study period should be held firm against interruptions from television, e-mail, telephone, irresponsible acquaintances, or "fluff" reading.

Two Minneapolis boys each had an IQ of 110 when they began as high school freshmen. John established his place and time for homework. Clement fooled around with friends; he went skating, hunting, and hiking, then used whatever time was left to do homework. Clement dropped out of school at the end of his sophomore year, but John plugged through his high school and college homework, and then enrolled for a master's degree in business administration. Later he completed his doctorate and became a financial leader in St. Paul.

Whether you are a student, rancher, or salesperson, build the habit of a regular study time period to advance your lifelong learning. This habit will shorten your road to success.

Build Habits of Perseverance

The student or worker who gives up as soon as roadblocks appear will miss the reward of satisfying success. Roadblocks will always be there.

The immortal John Milton became famous not by traveling an easy path, but by enduring poverty, imprisonment, ill health, public scorn, and blindness. His habit of persistence, never giving up, earned for him the recognition of being one of England's greatest literary geniuses.

It was said in ancient times that all roads led to Rome, but some highways were hilly, some had washed-out bridges, and some were guarded by overzealous legionnaires. It can now be said that all roads lead to success, but these highways, too, are guarded by discouragement, distractions, and often by ferocious dog-eat-dog competition. If you give up, if you are easily discouraged or fainthearted, failure will follow. But if you build habits of persistence so strong that nothing can turn you back, success will be yours.

When your habit of persistence meets an immovable object, you can go around, go over, dig under, tunnel through, take an alternate route, or find a way to make the immovable object movable. An old army saying humorously admonishes that if you come to an obstacle, move it. If you can't move it, paint it. If you can't paint it, salute it and carry on.

You will find that there are always roadblocks between you and success. Often the roadblock in your way, which is negative, can be turned into a positive. When rocks block your road, be sure that you don't miss the opportunity to use them as a bridge for the washout down the road.

Focus on the Positive

It is said that Samuel Clemens made less than perfect marks on his early mathematics examinations. He refused to consider the missed problems as failures. They served as experiments toward a better score. Once when he missed three out of ten and got a grade of seventy, barely passing, he quipped to friends that odds of seven to three were good in any horse race. Samuel Clemens — also known as Mark Twain — was right. He was accentuating the positive.

Avoid giving undue attention to mistakes. Instead, focus all of your energy on your successes. Use wrong answers, missteps, and other stumbles on the road to success simply as "experiments" toward a better end.

Build the Habit of Finishing Strong

Jesse Owens, Robert "Bob" Matthias, and Bruce Jenner all built one habit that led to their Olympic successes: the habit of finishing strong. At the end of a mile race, it's that final sprint that breaks the tape first. Then, according to the King of Sweden, there was "the greatest athlete in the world," Jim Thorpe. Thorpe always finished strong, being the only man to win the pentathlon and decathlon, and the first in history to kick a 48-yard field goal, which he accomplished while leading Carlisle Institute to victory over Harvard. Thorpe was the first president of the National Football League. As his teammate said of this Cherokee Native American, "he not only played on the team, he was the team." The trainers of winning race horses — Secretariat, Seattle Slough, and Affirmed — all said that winning by a neck or a length depends on that last ounce of energy.

All college students start even at the beginning on the first day of classes. Those who persist forge toward the front during the first quarter or semester. Some drop out before midterms. Others fall away through the years until only the strong finishers march in the June commencement four years later. Not only do the strong finishers complete their bachelor's degrees, but also the most determined, strongest finishers will go ahead to earn the master's and the doctorate.

The same rule holds for the world of work. Henry Ford was discouraged when he had his first automobile only half finished, but he had built habits of completing every task. When he designed mass production by assembly line, the lines would not flow. But he overcame all difficulties and finished strong to make a good, inexpensive "people's" car.

After a series of failures with steam-powered boats, Robert Fulton completed the *Clermont* in 1807. It had been nicknamed "Fulton's Folly" by every fence-sitting, straw-chewing wag in sight. Because he built a strong finishing habit before he built the *Clermont*, his smoke-belching contraption revolutionized navigation on the Hudson.

A little poem from McGuffey's Reader stresses habits for a strong finish: If a task is once begun/Never leave it till it's done./Be the labor great or small/Do it well, or not at all.

Things to Do

You are the sum of your habits. You can develop habits of thinking the right thoughts, being positive, enjoying your work, and seeing yourself as a winner. Emotionally, you can control your moods and your outlook on life. You can avoid extreme overreacting and bite your tongue when you are tempted to tell off your associates. Your health habits are vital. Build, develop, and improve the kind of habits that affect your health, health that is indispensable to success.

Habits can be consciously built, revised, or broken. If you wish to be successful in life, build the system of habits that will make for the greatest possible achievement in your chosen endeavor. Following are some activities to help you.

1. Make a list of your mental attitudes. Determine whether these habitual attitudes are leading you toward the success that you have chosen.
2. List all of the advantages and disadvantages of your present job or course of study. Focus on the advantages to you and to other people. Think about the real significance of your work to your community and to your country.
3. List the education institutions and other organizations that offer courses which could lead to advancement in your chosen profession. Evaluate the offerings.

4. Evaluate your present status with regard to your professional and personal growth plans. Where are you going? How can you get there? What special resources are needed?
5. List the sources of financial aid, which could help you to reach your lifelong learning goals.
6. Grade your habits for success on a checklist. Start with the ones listed on the chart on the following page and add other positive habits that best fit you.

GRADE YOUR HABITS

HABITS	YOUR GRADE				
	F	D	C	B	A
1. Starting early					
2. Enjoying your work					
3. Believing in your ability					
4. Scheduling time and place for work at home					
5. Organizing tools, supplies, equipment					
6. Avoiding distractions					
7. Stressing the positive					
8. Persisting toward a goal					
8. Making a strong finish					
10. Controlling your temper					
11. Avoiding unfair judgments					
12. Speaking well of others					
AVERAGE GRADE:					

CHAPTER SIX

How to Manage Yourself for Success

As our explorers and voyagers sail past Venus, Mars, Jupiter, and Saturn, they find no evidence of the human species. As far as we actually know at this time, Homo sapiens could be the highest order of life among billions of suns and planets.

The humanoid creature stands at the top of all life. We manage our own lives and the lives of all plants and animals. The lower animals follow their instincts; the human being uses observation, experimentation, reasoning, judgment, and makes decisions. Psychologists question whether any animal consciously plans for tomorrow. They certainly do not plan for "Social Security."

Garter snakes slither, coyotes howl, canaries sing, and wild geese migrate, just as their ancestors did thousands of generations ago. Homo sapiens discarded his first hatchet in favor of bronze, which he replaced with iron that he coupled to electricity. He hurled machines into outer space. Poke a high school senior and he or she may laugh, swear, strike, feel sorry for you, or plan to slip some cayenne pepper into your soup. Self-management is a human prerogative. It is a license without limits.

What Is Self-Management?

Self-management, simply defined, is a conscious process of choosing one's experiences. Horses make no plans for tomorrow, but you store food, invest in retirement accounts, and buy life insurance. Self-management is uniquely human. It is at once our greatest privilege and greatest responsibility.

Socrates said, "Know thyself." Your first step in self-management is to understand what you have to manage. Am I physical? Am I mental? Am I emotional? Am I social? Am I spiritual? Am I all of these? Am I static or ever-changing?

The self that you manage at five years of age is different from the self that you manage at 20 or at 80. Your privilege, or right, to self-management changes with age and experience. Self-management is virtually zero at birth. Someone else manages feeding and sleeping schedules, diaper changes, and room temperatures. We cannot communicate too well. It's difficult to be a baby.

Teenagers often clash with parents over what they eat, when they watch television, and how they drive the family car. They are beginning to assert the right of self-management. Then when the child reaches complete maturity, he or she can make decisions without any external imposition.

Self-management involves a scrambled, interrelated combination of physical, mental, emotional, social, and other attributes that are ever changing. To succeed in self-management, diagnose yourself as Socrates advised, and then prescribe the experiences that will be best for you and others. Self-management for success is essential. It requires concentrated effort. It certainly is not easy, and some specific aspects merit attention.

For example, managing your physical self is vital to success. It involves health and safety, even survival. Your health can be maintained, and it can be improved. At any given time in your life, your body is a composite of many systems, such as circulation, digestion, oxygen intake and control, skeletal stability, neural function, muscle tone, and glandular secretion. Your self-management job is to keep all of these systems functioning in balanced coordination. No system or set of systems is ever perfect, and so your job is to improve each system toward maximum performance.

To have all systems performing at their best, you need to know what to do and then to do it. For example, a buyer in a department store loved to eat rich chocolate bars for lunch. But they made her feel slightly ill and gave her an afternoon headache that interfered with her work. By force of will, she changed that sweet-tooth habit to a lunch of fresh fruit and vegetables. She lost weight, felt better, had more energy, avoided headaches, and became more efficient on her job. She carried her knowledge into action that resulted in success.

To achieve success, you must have concern for your own safety. As our mechanized society becomes more complex, men and women are in greater danger. I lost three close working associates in separate commercial airplane disasters. Radiation fallout threatens mankind through air, water, milk supply, and other sources. Highway accidents kill more people each year than were lost in the Vietnam War. This list of dangers could be extended endlessly. A world in motion is a hazardous world. No matter how healthy you may be, no matter how well you have organized your course of study or your business or your family relations, a one-second mistake on the highway can destroy everything. Self-management of your own safety is vital to your success and the success of all who depend on you.

To best manage your safety, you must know the sources of danger. Then you must act to avoid the danger. The best protection requires avoiding your own mistakes and watching out for the mistakes of others. Applied to highway safety, you would not only drive carefully, but you would drive defensively, to avert the mistakes of others. Similarly, the best self-defense is to be someplace else. It is best to avoid dangerous areas, to avoid going out alone at night, and to avoid secluded or isolated locations. It is especially important that you be aware of your surroundings and alert to what is going on around you.

When you self-manage for good health and safety, success is within your reach. But if you fritter away your health or take unnecessary risks that result in accidents, the success you have hoped for turns to defeat and despair.

How to Manage Your Mental Self

To manage your mental self, you must begin by following Socrates' advice and diagnose your mental capabilities and opportunities. People differ in the mental power that they inherit.

They also differ in their possibilities for intellectual growth. Fairly recently, psychologists have discovered that there are many kinds of intelligence.

Chapter Four dealt with lifelong learning. Keep on learning for life. Mental management for success demands that you seize upon every opportunity for mental growth. But there's more to mental self-management than a commitment to lifelong learning.

In managing your mental self for success, it is important to understand that your mental self is in no way isolated from your physical self. The mental and the physical aspects of your total personality are so intricately intertwined that they can be separated only by verbal description. They function as a unit. The physical brain is as essential to thought as the gun is to the ammunition. Your mental self is totally involved when you physically tie knots in a rope. The physical and mental selves are as inseparable as the heads and tails of a coin.

Even though the strongest of cords bind the physical and mental selves together, the mental self can be measured and expressed as an intelligence quotient. These measures distribute themselves on the normal probability curve that we discussed earlier. Psychologists such as Terman recognized the degrees of intelligence before later psychologists, such as Guilford, recognized a wide range in the kinds of intelligence. Any large class of students will vary widely in amount and types of intelligence. Some may be higher in one area but lower in another. Some will be stronger in mathematics, but miserable in drawing and verbal skills. Still others may be highly proficient in social and human relationships but near the bottom of the scale in English composition. Indeed, an early attempt to recognize the types of intelligence was to divide students into verbal and nonverbal groups. The verbal students were academic and prepared for college. The nonverbal would excel in manipulation, best suiting them for the trades.

All of the types of intelligence you possess can be strengthened. Your task in mental self-management is to discover your intelligence strengths, develop them to the fullest, and work to strengthen those areas in which you feel weakness. All types of intelligence are vehicles for success.

How to Manage the Emotional Self

Emotions are the mainspring of human action. They are the drives that carry you toward your goal. Your self-management of emotions for success requires some understanding of your emotional behavior.

Some psychologists, such as Woodworth and Thorndike, leaned toward the pleasure-pain theory of emotions, believing that behavior which results in pleasure will be repeated, but behavior which results in pain will be avoided. Neurological psychologists have located the main seat of emotions in the limbic system of the brain's thalamus. Endocrine psychologists, such as Berman, have pointed to the glands as regulators of human behavior.

Physiological psychologists have pointed to the hypothalamus and the reward centers in the brain, such as the medial forebrain bundle, as controlling pleasant responses to stimuli such as sex, food, and social contact. In terms of biology, we know that the digestive processes, heartbeat, and epinephrine (adrenaline) flow, and a whole range of physiological responses are affected by emotions such as anger and fear by way of the sympathetic branch of the autonomic nervous system, the branch of our nervous system that controls our automatic responses.

The James-Lange theory of emotions implied that bodily action and posture arouse emotion, rather than emotion being the cause of action. We see a bear, we run, and only then do we feel the emotion. In other words, we are afraid because we run, and we are angry because we assume the posture of fighting and strike. Later psychologists recognize a circular effect: We run because we fear, and the more we run, the more we fear. Singer and Schacter said that it is the interpretation of our bodily states — our physiology — within the context in which those bodily states are occurring that determines the emotions we experience.

The developing science of psychology has made great strides toward discovering what emotions are and how they affect behavior. The important conclusion to remember is that each individual has a vast array of emotional responses and that these responses can be controlled. They can be controlled, channeled, and directed toward successful behavior. Men and women succeed and fail according to the way they master their emotions.

Great changes in human and social affairs are brought about by emotional drives. Carrie Nation never heard of an IQ test, but she took her hatchet and smashed saloons, bringing the Women's Christian Temperance Union into prominence and providing Kansas with the reputation of being "the dry state." It was likely that George Washington Carver may have had more scientific ability than Martin Luther King, Jr. but Reverend King had a dream, a dream that made him the leader of civil rights causes in America. John Paul Jones did not know enough about marine logistics to understand that his *Bonhomme Richard* was hopelessly outgunned by the British *Serapis*, so he shouted, "I have not yet begun to fight!" Then he proceeded to defeat Britain's superior force. Emotion, rather than reason, won the day.

TIPS FOR SUCCESS

- Don't smoke.

- Eat a sensible diet, and don't skip breakfast.

- Avoid excessive caffeine and alcohol.

- Get enough sleep.

- Fix the problem, instead of fixing blame.

- Listen more than you talk.

- Don't be a victim.

- Learn how to relax.

- But don't become a couch potato. Exercise!

You cannot ignore your emotions. They are there. They must be dealt with. They must be managed. Fortunately, you can marshal them toward success in social, marital, financial, political, personal, artistic, and scientific areas. Success is yours when you make your emotions heel and sit at your command. Count to ten before you take offense, for example. Take a course in martial arts and learn to meditate. Relax. Start by learning to relax all of your muscles. Control your breathing. Then relax your mind. Use mental imagery: See yourself looking at ease and relaxed. If your body is relaxed, and you are breathing slowly and deeply, your subconscious mind will think that all is well — and it will be. This is the basis for a major psychotherapeutic technique called systematic desensitization.

When you manage your emotions, you assume greater control of your drive toward success.

How to Manage Your Social Self

While an occasional lone wolf can hunt by itself, most wolves — and people — need companionship. Wolves need other wolves. People need other people. "No man is an island." You are born into a family. You attend school in classes. You marry not only your spouse, but also your in-laws. You are not a lone wolf. You work with others on the job. You worship with others in your church, mosque, temple, or synagogue. You are a social being.

To be successful in any line of endeavor, you must manage your social self and get along with people. More workers lose their jobs because they quarrel with their supervisors and other workers than because they lack job skills. On the other hand, workers become supervisors, and supervisors become vice presidents, because they know how to work harmoniously and productively with associates.

Dale Carnegie wrote *How to Win Friends and Influence People.* It became an all-time best-seller because he emphasized managing the social self. Psychologists and sociologists have written thick books with esoteric terms about social forces, social interrelationships, and social values. This section avoids the language of sociology in favor of common sense.

Briefly, you will be successful in managing your social self if you . . .

- are a giving person,
- speak well of your associates,
- listen with empathy, and
- evaluate your social self, making adjustments as needed.

It may be "more blessed to give than to receive," but probably 90% of the general population consists of takers, rather than givers. You cannot be successful and outstanding if you merely follow the crowd. Be different. Be distinctive. Add values to your social relationships. Be a giving person.

To manage your social self as a giver rather than a taker, develop a habit of feeling pleasure when you give. Give your spouse the choice cut. Give your children time and attention. Surprise your parents or your teacher or your professor with kindly, thoughtful words and acts. Spend some of your valuable leisure time in projects that involve the whole family. If you are working on an assembly line or in an office, take over for a friend who is ill or troubled. Bring your friends some carrots or a rose that grew in your garden. Send a greeting card and go to see an associate who is in the hospital.

If you think in terms of giving as a means of being successful, the two concepts seem to be in conflict. They are not. In managing your social self to help others, the more you give the more you will get. Andrew Carnegie became immortal because he felt it was a disgrace to die rich. Your own self-interest is best served when you give. Be a giver, not a taker.

In social management, speak well of your associates. Avoid gossip. Look for the good qualities of your friends and verbalize them. You may recall that old stanza: "There is so much good in the worst of us/And so much bad in the best of us/That it behooves none of us/To talk about the rest of us."

Sir Francis Bacon said, "Discretion of speech is more than eloquence." Elbert Hubbard agreed when he said, "If you work for a man . . . speak well of him."

If you tear down a person's character by speech, you are guilty of slander even if what you say is true. If you maliciously attempt to injure the other person, you are legally at fault and the injured person can initiate legal action against you. Remember what Shakespeare wrote: "Who steals my purse steals trash, but he that filches from me my good name makes me poor indeed."

Turning to the positive, try to find assets in the other person that you can honestly compliment. You will be helping yourself socially, and you will help your associate personally. Tell a person that he or she is kind, and that individual will try to live up to your expectation. In all cases avoid flattery, and be sincere.

In managing your social self as a means of attaining desired successes, it is necessary to be outgoing, rather than introspective. Excluding hermits and sailors marooned on desert islands, the people in this crowded world must be outgoing and sensitive to the needs, interests, and ideas of other persons.

Did you ever attend a party and have someone bore you with a 20-minute lecture on his own aches, pains, financial reverses, family troubles, parking tickets, and penalties related to Form 1040? Did you enjoy the conversation? Of course not.

The best way to be outgoing is to be sincerely interested in another person's likes and dislikes. Just ask a few impersonal questions. Will the Yankees make it to the Series again this year? What is new and exciting at your job? What are your favorite class subjects? Movies? Television programs? Then listen with attention. This compliments your social partner.

The art of conversation may be waning in a media-driven age, but if you ask questions about special interests and listen, your social partner will hardly notice how little you have said and will rate you as a top conversationalist. Being truly interested in the welfare of others includes being sensitive and considerate.

How to Manage Your Spiritual Self

As far as we know, man is the only creation that searches for a Creator beyond the earth's horizon. H.G. Wells is sometimes given credit for saying, "Man is incurably religious." Since the beginning of the human species, its members have made stone images, set up icons, built temples, delivered homage, and prayed for help from a god or gods.

In the light of expanding knowledge, our concepts of the deity are always changing. The concept of God has evolved in the mind of man. To the scientist, God may be universal law; to the poet, beauty of nature; and to the theologian, the Creator of man.

Even though psychologist J.B. Watson said he could not find souls in a test tube, his later writings hinted something beyond cold behaviorism. Carl Menninger, the world-famous psychiatrist, looks on spiritual forces as the individual's balance wheel of adjustment.

Modern psychologists are rather agreed that men and women are free to plot their own spiritual course. The individual chooses his or her own spiritual attitudes and concepts. These can be directed toward success or failure.

Oral Roberts is an example of a man who managed his own spiritual development. After he collapsed with tuberculosis on the basketball floor, missed an assassin's bullet, and escaped from a mob in Australia, he built a great university, preached to millions in person and by television, and planned one of the great hospital healing centers in mid-America. Reverend Roberts managed his spiritual self through many crises to become eminently successful.

Reverend Roberts sets forth a concept of seed-faith. Plant a seed, and it will grow and multiply. Build your faith, he believes, and no worthwhile tasks are too great. He believes in and has proven an outstanding example of accomplishment unlimited through managing his spiritual self. His three principles are sound psychologically and theologically. They are:

1. God is your source.
2. Give that it may be given to you.
3. Expect a miracle.

Anyone who stands in the 200-foot-high Prayer Tower with its eternal flame, and the thousand mirrors reflecting the blue sky by day and the stars by night, must believe that miracles can happen. They did in Tulsa. This unique and beautiful edifice overlooking Oral Roberts University and the city of Tulsa is a living testimony to the thousands who had the faith needed to bring it about. If you have faith in your dreams of success, you can bring them about.

How to Manage Your Problem-Solving Self

In Western culture, we tend to blame others when things don't seem to be going well. In Japan, the focus is on solving a problem, rather than on fixing blame. The successful person uses problem-solving techniques to reach success.

To solve a problem, do not just jump into the fray and start *doing* things. First, state or define the problem. Know exactly what the limits are: What are you trying to accomplish? Exactly what is the problem you are trying to solve?

Second, you should survey the situation. Have others experienced similar problems? How did they resolve their situation? Make a listing of possible solutions. Also, try to anticipate the hazards — the pitfalls — if any, which may be involved in adopting the different possible solutions.

Third, use the most powerful techniques available to analyze the data you have gathered. Let experts help you.

Fourth, decide which of the many possible solutions to try. Remember that you can always change your mind!

Finally, evaluate the results. Recycle as necessary.

Things to Do

The person who tries to succeed without first managing him- or herself is bound to fail. Self-management emerges over time as the individual matures. But all self-management behaviors are learned. If they aren't learned well, they must be relearned. For the highest success in life, each individual must manage his or her physical, mental, emotional, social, and spiritual self. Following are some activities that can prove useful.

1. Rate yourself somewhere between 0 and 100 on the scale of self-management. What can you do in order to be able to rate yourself higher?
2. List areas of your life not mentioned in this chapter where self-management is vital.
3. Select half a dozen highly successful men and women of your acquaintance. Observe the ways in which they manage their own lives.
4. List five ways to better manage your own physical, mental, emotional, social, and spiritual self.

CHAPTER SEVEN

How to Manage Your Surroundings — People and Things

Heredity and environment make you what you are. You cannot choose your heredity, but you can choose your environment — at least as an adult. You can choose to live in Nome, Possum Run, Key West, Rattlesnake Gulch, Guam, or Brooklyn. You may binge on pastries and sugar, or you may choose vegetables and protein. You can read drivel and violence, or choose the "hundred best books."

Your success will depend on how wisely you choose your environment. Yes, you can manage your surroundings. Psychologists tell us that people react to stimuli. So choose the stimuli that will propel you toward your goal of success. Managing the people and things about you does this.

How to Manage People

Managing people is both an art and a science. It is an art and a science that you can and must learn. The proposition really is not *whether* you manage people, but *how well*. Then the question arises, how long do you have to manage people? From earliest childhood to the end of life, the extent to which you manage your relationships with people around you indicates the extent of your life's success.

Nature is not stupid. It gave a baby a technique for managing people anywhere within earshot. If the diaper pin sticks her, she cries. If he's hungry, he cries. If she's wet and itchy, she cries. This cry brings the nurse or the mother with a remedy. The baby's cry is cash. It's the currency of the realm. With a disturbing cry, the baby buys what he or she wants. The baby is managing people.

At two years old, the tiny toddler is managing people in different ways. A toddler can still use the minted crying coins but has added some newly printed greenbacks. Take the tantrum, for instance. If a toddler doesn't get to knock the syrup bottle off the shelf at the grocery store, he or she falls to the floor in a fit: a tantrum. If the toddler gets attention, he has managed his mother or father or auntie.

At sixteen, Junior follows a blizzard to the driveway and imitates a snowplow. It just happens that the Prom is coming up, and Junior could use the keys to the family car. He is employing a managerial technique on his father.

All through life boys and girls, men and women, must manage the people around them. Suppose the crying baby, the howling toddler, the snow-shoveling teenager keeps managing people and becomes president of a big company. Now he is in the big league and must make further successes by managing people.

The company president truly must manage in many dimensions at once. The president must lead the board of directors to keep harmony and direct their efforts toward company growth. He or she must manage and lead all employees of the company so that productivity will be increased. The president must manage the buying public through advertising so that more widgets and dingbats will be sold. And the president must manage government regulators and company researchers so that he can keep peace, avoid litigation, and advance the company.

People management, like loyalty, is not a one-way street. From the time that a child learns that a smile will buy more than a tantrum, people management becomes a process of mutuality. You give and you get. And the old rule holds true that the more you give, the more you get. Jackie Robinson had something to give baseball, so he managed his manager and became the first African American to play in the Big League.

Junior got the keys to the family car by shoveling snow, thereby showing Dad he was responsible enough to be trusted with the car. And by helping Mom with the evening dishes, he knew she would be glad to iron the wrinkles out of his shirt and supply enough cash for his sweetheart's corsage.

How to Be a Successful Leader

Being a leader requires one to be true to one's own ideals and, at the same time, to be sufficiently flexible so as to be able to perform many specialized duties and functions for a group or organization in a continuously changing environment. Successful leaders meet the expectations, aspirations, needs, and demands of the group. The successful leader is:

- *Sensitive* to the feelings of others: considerate, helpful, responsive, and friendly.
- *Loyal* to his or her ideas and ideals — but respectful of the beliefs, rights, and dignity of others.
- *Strong* in terms of self-confidence — but with the ability to identify easily with co-workers, both supervisors and those supervised.
- *Consistent* in attitude: generous, humble, modest, fair, and honest in dealing with others.
- *Enthusiastic* about his or her work.
- *Interested* in improvement — and in getting a job done quickly and in the most economical, efficient, and correct manner.
- *Aware* of the need to avoid envy, jealously, and other counterproductive feelings.
- *Willing* to take the blame for his or her own mistakes — and to make things right.
- *Firm* but not stubborn — certain to give co-workers the benefit of the doubt and the advantage whenever possible.

Learn to Delegate

Many who aspire to leadership are unwilling or reluctant to deputize or delegate. Others willingly delegate responsibilities but fail to give the necessary authority to get results. Still others will delegate authority and responsibility and then attempt to abdicate their own ultimate responsibility for what happens. No leader can say, "The responsibility is yours," and then forget it. The amount of follow-up is a function of the amount and type of work and of the individual to whom the responsibility has been delegated. Bruce, who joined the company two days ago, will require more follow-ups than will Gary, who has been with the organization for 20 years.

The leader is primarily responsible for making things happen through the efforts of people. Only when he or she perceives this facet of the position will he or she be truly successful. To be a successful leader, you must possess the ability and willingness to delegate. You can't and should not try to do it all yourself.

Learn to Communicate

As human beings, we have a strong instinct for self-preservation and security. We human beings are conservative, security-seeking creatures and resist change almost instinctively. We may be in a rut, but we really know that rut! We are adjusted to it. There are no twists or turns to our rut with which we are not familiar. But, to paraphrase Will Rogers, if you get on a familiar track and just sit on it, eventually you will get run over. Leaders are managers, often initiators, of change. They must be the train on the track.

If, as leader, you want to change something you *must* use effective communication. Even then, remember, while a child can change the shape of an inflatable, plastic globe by opening a valve and squeezing, it is very difficult to change the world in a day, even if you are a great communicator, because there will be great resistance to change and therefore little inclination to listen to ideas which would change the present state of affairs. You certainly won't be able to get things done without really effective communication skills.

Recall Aristotle's maxim, "It is not enough to know what to say, it is necessary also to know how to say it." Effective leadership is impossible for the person who lacks the ability to express ideas.

16 Keys to Effective Communication

Following are 16 keys to effective communication that can help you become successful as a communicator.

1. Speak wisely and well. The following anonymous lines offer a bit of good advice:

> If wisdom's ways you wisely seek,
> Five things you will observe with care,
> Of whom you speak, to whom to speak,
> And how and when and where.

2. Develop a liking for people. Whether you speak to one person or a thousand, they can tell in a split second whether or not you are eager to share good ideas with them or if your words come only from your lips, not from your heart.

3. Keep informed. This task is not easy and often means sacrificing leisure time. But you will be a much more effective supervisory leader if you keep abreast of what is going on in education in general and in supervision in particular; in the social and professional organizations to which you belong; and on the local, national, and international scenes.

4. Go and keep going. If you belong to an organization or group, be informed and play an active role in its meetings and programs. Above all else, make your voice heard. Remember that unexpressed ideas are of no more value than the kernels in a nut before it is cracked.

5. Think before you speak. As noted in so many other places in this book, take a few seconds to organize your thoughts, rather than blurting out a gush of words. Clear thinking must precede clear speaking. A moment's thinking is worth an hour in garbled words.

6. Keep the other fellow in mind. Try to understand the other person's point of view. Again, develop empathy. Avoid sarcasm,

barbed remarks, and personal insults, for the use of these weapons is an indication of weakness, not of strength.

7. Display a calm manner and clear, sound thinking in the midst of heated discussion. Let these qualities be manifest in your tone of voice, your facial expression or posture, and in the volume and rate of your speaking.

8. Concentrate on your message, not on yourself. Focus attention on what you have to say and you automatically will forget yourself. Fear of being misunderstood, or even laughed at, taken with a grain of salt, will be put in the background.

9. Collect material for your discussions. Look for facts and "slices of life" that can be used in your talks. Tear out items from newspapers and magazines and underscore passages in books; collect materials that your audience may wish to see, rather than hear about, that pertain to your topic. Jot down your ideas on index cards or keep a small notebook with you.

10. Be brief and precise. Do not bite off more than you can chew or more than your listeners want to hear. Omit long and unnecessary explanations. Select your point and go to it. Use short sentences. Be economical in your use of words, never using three or four where one will do.

11. Make nervousness work for you. Most people are a bit frightened when speaking before a group. The beginner especially may be fearful when addressing a first faculty meeting or parent association. But a little fear can be an asset. It can sharpen your talks and make them sparkle. Before you begin, consciously relax your muscles and quietly look around at your audience for 10 or 15 seconds.

12. Be enthusiastic. Recall that the word *enthusiasm* comes from two Greek words, *en* and *theos*, meaning "in God." So let the divine spark show through when you want to communicate constructive ideas. But do not confuse enthusiasm with bombast, wild gestures, or emotional display. You can be enthusiastic in a whisper or without moving so much as a finger.

13. Let gestures help you. They can be an outward expression of inner convictions and add dimension to your words. A wave of

the arm, a raising of the eyebrow, shrugging the shoulders, nodding the head — all can serve to underscore your words.

14. Communicate with your eyes. "Eye communication" means more than "eye contact." It implies looking directly at your listeners and actually talking with your eyes. Sweep the audience gently with a warm, friendly gaze, allowing your glance to rest here and there for a brief second or two. It is far easier to know whether you are making your point if you look at your listeners, rather than at the floor or ceiling.

15. Be a good listener. Learn from the thoughts and ideas of others. Recall from Epictetus: "Nature has given to man one tongue, but two ears, that we may hear from others twice as much as we speak."

16. Know when to stop. Make your point and sit down.

> ## TIPS FOR SUCCESS
>
> - Don't just be on time; be early.
> - Be assertive.
> - Listen to others.
> - Solve a problem; don't sell a solution.
> - Appreciate human differences.
> - Know what you want and how to manage your surroundings to get it.

Simple, Concrete Language

Specialists in the language arts, in psychology, in supervision, and in communication theory have listed the principles of effective communication. Those who are receiving the communication, be they listeners or readers, appreciate:

- Specific examples that: a) involve the familiar, b) use specific description, c) present colorful analogies, or d) give statistical data.
- Clear terminology that is free of superlatives, trite expressions, repetition, and phrases such as "et cetera" or "and so forth."

Listeners dislike statements such as, "Of course, it's only my opinion . . . ." Of course it is your opinion; that is why you are expressing it. Naturally "it seems to me," or you would not be saying it. They also dislike punch-pulling phrases such as "more or less," or "to a greater or lesser degree."

Listeners and readers appreciate communication that is grammatically sure-footed and easy to understand. Sentences usually should not exceed 20 words. When a sentence begins to crumble under its own weight, then it's too ponderous. Break the thought into smaller chunks, and your idea will be clear.

In summary, successful communication is: conversational, specific, picturesque, clear, and to the point.

How to Be a Successful Salesperson

Yes, you can use sales savvy to go after a career in the local department store, but that's not my point. All successful individuals "sell" — themselves, their ideas, their programs.

The word *sell* unfortunately seems to imply pressure for self-interest. That's the wrong way to sell. When young sales agents focus on their own commissions rather than providing first-rate service to their customers or clients, they fail.

Cater to the needs of your "customer" (friend, teacher, student, supervisor). Make that person stand tall, as opposed to boosting your own ego by pulling someone else down. Abraham Lincoln said, "You cannot strengthen the weak by weakening the strong." Pull everyone up.

When you "sell" something to people, when you manage them, you can be most successful by focusing first on their self-interest. Forget about selling your customer a new suit until you have asked what he wants in the way of size, pattern, color, and fabric. First, satisfy him that you have his best interest — his needs and wants — at heart. Then your sale will follow. When you make the client happy, the client will make you happy. This is the key to success.

With good people management, good salesmanship, who wins? When Junior helped his mother with the dishes, when the company president made the best widget — everybody won! Failure spawns losers; success makes everyone a winner.

If everybody has to manage people, you will question whether everyone can be a good salesperson. Do some observing. Watch the young man wooing his future mate. Notice how he preens his hair, polishes his shoes, says polite things, rushes around his car to open the door, and takes her to the "in" places. She, too, does a selling job. She splashes on exotic perfumes, dresses appropriately, and keeps him waiting just the respectable amount of time.

It may surprise students to know that the best teachers are masters at selling. The best teachers know how to begin every lesson with stimulation, which leads to motivation. They begin with the child's interests and explain a confusing and changing world. Teachers are salespeople? Yes! They are the greatest salespeople in the world. Of course, there are exceptions. There are poor teachers. A few may care more for themselves than the children. These poor salespersons mark their students low and flunk in their own profession. On the other hand, the teacher who gives the most, sells lessons the best, knows the subject matter, and loves working with the students, achieves the highest success and satisfactions.

Consider the "sales" job of Anne Sullivan, teacher of deaf and blind Helen Keller. Anne Sullivan herself had suffered from partial blindness, poverty, and loss of family. But she learned how to sell her lessons to the blind. Her student, Helen Keller, was lost in a cellar of eternal darkness. But with ingenuity, patience, and endless love, Anne taught Helen by touch to "feel" her way into a world of light and excitement. Helen Keller later wrote of her teacher, "The most important day I remember in my life is the one on which my teacher . . . came to me. I am filled with wonder when I consider the immeasurable contrast between the two lives . . . ."

It is not only teachers who manage people in the classroom; it also is students. The student who wishes to be successful in the classroom manages the teacher and other students. To manage the teacher, the student attends to assignments, enthusiastically follows directions, avoids distractions, and in every way cooperates to complete class projects. Young people are very sensitive to their peers. In every class there are leaders who set standards of behavior for other members of the class. They are managing people, selling their way of life. Every student in the class, to some degree, manages all others. George Gregory, in his book, *The Natural Laws of Success*, stresses mutualism in the classroom: The teacher gives factual material and guidance; the students give orderly attention with disciplined learning.

Students who learn best to manage their teachers, fellow students, and others are learning to get along successfully with people. Getting along with people is the first step to success in family life, business, government, and leisurely sociability.

How to Be a Successful Supervisor

Teachers and students manage people in the classroom. And in business and industry supervisors and workers manage each other. (This is true also of teachers and principals, principals and superintendents.) To increase productivity, the supervisor can throw away the stick of threatening control and supply the carrot of satisfaction for a worker's needs and desires. Supervisors can increase business productivity by recognizing each worker as an important person and as an improving company producer.

Workers, like students, appreciate recognition. They have wants and needs. The supervisor who shows interest in, and concern for, these needs is contributing to the company's successful production.

Just as students manage teachers, so should workers manage supervisors. Workers can please their supervisors by: 1) being early, rather than arriving barely on time, 2) doing quality work, 3) increasing output, and 4) demonstrating positive human relations, getting along well with co-workers. Always find time to do successful things.

Words of wisdom from *Life's Little Instruction Book* by H. Jackson Brown, Jr. urge: "Don't say you don't have enough time. You have exactly the same number of hours per day that were given to Pasteur, Michelangelo, Mother Teresa, Helen Keller, Leonardo da Vinci, Thomas Jefferson, and Albert Einstein."

How to Manage "Things"

Both children and adults must manage the "things" around them. The word *things* is all inclusive. Whether you manage roller blades, bicycles, or fish tanks as a child or manage automobiles, houses, or computer systems as an adult, you still have to cope with a world of things and conditions. These things and conditions may be man-made or natural. They even may be forms of animal life.

Managing the Natural Environment. Since the beginning of time, humankind has stood in awe or has run when confronted with a lightning flash, a whirling tornado, or a crushing hurricane. Out of the hidden past have come legends of poisonous dragons, man-eating animals, and bewitching fowls of the air. Bit by bit those dangers have been controlled.

All people must help to manage the environment around them. Management of the environment becomes increasingly important as the number of people increases. A century ago, wild prairies, forests, and animals were so abundant that it seemed they could never be exhausted. Now we are elbowing into the last remaining sanctuaries of wildlife. Rainforests are losing ground. We must manage or lose our natural heritage.

The Exxon Valdez oil spill will live forever in infamy in pristine Alaska. To be successful in managing our natural world, we have become more concerned about fish-killing chemicals in our lakes and rivers, irritants in our atmosphere, and soil pollutants that endanger our food supply. The world of insects has contained a threat to the human species. At this point, the race between insects and mankind's survival seems to be in a dead heat. Microscopic bacteria, viruses, germs, and defective genes are latecomer threats.

Our management of the natural world will determine our success, even our very existence.

Managing the Human-Made Environment. With more than 50,000 people killed each year on our highways, it would seem that our safety management leaves much to be desired. Public health management, however, has been far more successful. People are living longer, thanks to researchers such as Jonas Salk, who discovered a vaccine for poliomyelitis. In spite of cancer, heart disease, and a few other killers, our management of human health has been highly successful, with more and more individuals living to full maturity.

Modern high school students have to manage learning devices that their grandparents never dreamed of. Video recorders, laser discs, a variety of projectors, films, computers with interactive programming, programmed learning, sound recording and projection, locating and accessing information on the Internet, photocopiers, word processors, arc welding in the machine shop, plastic and fiberglass rods for the pole vault, and microwave ovens for food service, are some of the "things" to be managed by students.

As an adult, each person has to manage a more complex and confusing world of inventions, gadgets, and systems. From the young couple selecting just the right engagement diamond to the laser surgeon, and the auto mechanic who now must deal with computerized automotive systems, the management of all of these ever more complicated and confusing things determines the degree of the individual's success.

In conclusion, you must manage other people and the world of things about you. The best way to manage people is to begin by identifying and serving their wants and desires. In this way your own needs will be best served and your objectives realized. This approach is master salesmanship. It is the way to success.

Managing the things of nature and human-made inventions is the key to success and sometimes to survival. In this area, success can mean satisfied living. Whether you dodge a careening car, avoid a water moccasin, go into a shelter before a tornado arrives, prepare for an earthquake, take your flu shots, install a smoke alarm, or invest in an individual retirement account, you are managing natural and human-made things.

If you manage your surroundings poorly, you will be the maker of your own failure. If you manage well, yours will be a life of happiness and success.

Things to Do

1. List the people in your life whom you must manage for their own good and for your success.
2. Jot down in priority order five ways in which you can best manage the people you have just named.
3. Determine in your own mind the best way of "selling" to bring about the greatest feeling of satisfaction to your clients and to you.
4. If excellent teachers rank high in selling skills, what about politicians, military officers, ministers, bank presidents, and parents? Name others.
5. In your community, how are you threatened by electrical/mechanical devices, animals or insects, weather conditions, or other factors? What can you do to better manage your environment?
6. Write down three things in your environment that you believe *you* can improve and state how you would go about it.

CHAPTER EIGHT

How to Manage Time

You were born without clothes, you could not focus your eyes, and you had neither the sense nor the physical coordination to come in out of the rain. One thing you had: time. Maybe a minute, maybe a dozen years, maybe three score and ten — nobody knew. But all of you, and everything that you could ever be, had to be squeezed into that indefinite span of time.

Time is a traveler, a vagabond, a gypsy, always going, never coming. The Bible tells us, "To every thing there is a season . . . a time to be born, and a time to die . . . ." (Ecclesiastes 3:1-2). In between being born and dying, there are many intervals of life that cradle successes.

Life is a series of intervals: baby, child, teenager, young adult, middle age, the golden age of the senior citizen and superannuated. Shakespeare sums up the intervals of life in his oft quoted "seven ages." Then there are intervals within intervals. The teenager may have several infatuations or "puppy love" affairs, and the adult may have more than one spouse and probably will have several jobs or career changes.

Your intervals of time are strung with golden moments. You can use each golden moment toward your goal of better marks, popularity, a successful marriage, job promotion, social enjoyment, personal adjustment, economic security, and spiritual satisfaction. If you fail to use a golden moment as it comes by, it is gone forever and you are bereft of that jewel in time. Successful living means living every moment as if it were your last. Make every moment and every day a golden step to the next interval of time. After all, time is all you have.

10 Rules for Successful Use of Time

Your golden moments of time will bring you success and satisfaction when you use them well. Following are 10 "rules" that you can follow to improve how you use your precious time.

1. Plan time to achieve your goals.
2. Tackle the hardest and most important tasks first.
3. Start your tasks early and quickly.
4. Strive for excellence, not perfection.
5. Enlist the support of others.
6. Schedule periods of rest or changes of activity.
7. Stay on track: Refuse to be interrupted.
8. Finish strong: complete your task.
9. Leave tomorrow's worry at the shop or office.
10. Delight in accomplishment . . . and relax.

Time for Your Goals

Goals are indispensable. They are your homing beacon, your north star. They keep you focused, on target. Never wander through life like the wolfhound that switches trails when a coyote crosses; then switches to follow a rabbit, a fox, and finally a little field mouse. Keep your star shining in full view.

List your lifetime goals. In what areas do you want to improve? Some areas you may want your list to include: mental, physical, social, spiritual, occupational, recreational, marital, economic, and personal. Add as many others as you like. Do you want to have a magnetic personality? Have more friends? See many parts of the world? If so, add these areas to your list of goals.

You know that you will never realize absolute psychological, physical, or social perfection, but you can reach milestones along the way. You reach those milestones in the flux of time. Unless you set time allotments for the attainments of goals, time will slip by on your blind side like a shadow in the night and leave you bereft and bare. You must use time effectively to reach each milestone along your route, leading toward your ultimate goals.

Make a time chart for your life's goals. Stay with any area, such as physical. What kind of physique do you want in one, five, 10, 20, or 30 years?

Suppose you are a teenager. Is your goal to grow to full potential height? Then lay off the junk food, cigarettes, and substance abuse.

Do you want to make the team? If so, plan time for practice, rest, time for relaxation and meditation, time for classes in several areas (including exercise), and time for a sensible diet. Do you want to enter middle age or the golden years with vigor, agility, and a slim, youthful appearance? Then take time for exercise, time for proper rest, and time for a sensible diet of wholesome foods.

Chart every goal within a framework of time. Each interval of time will move you closer to your goal. Remember, the pathway is gradual: "Inch by inch, anything's a cinch." And you will grow in strength. Recall how Hercules wrestled the giant, and every time he was thrown to the ground he got up with doubled strength. Just so, hour by hour, you can multiply your power.

Tackle the Toughest Tasks First

Are you a procrastinator? A dawdler? Do you put off, put off, and put off? Do you do your term paper on the last day of the semester and then have to stay up all night to finish it? Do you do what you feel like doing at the moment, instead of realizing what you should do? Are you lazy?

Thomas Jefferson at Monticello was the most successful landed baron of his age. Colleagues marveled at how he always had time for afternoon teas, political discussions, scientific study, educational planning, agriculture, and friendly visitation. They failed to recognize that he was a perfect example of someone who obeyed the second rule for successful use of time. Jefferson tackled his hardest and most important job first — usually before others were awake. He wrote some of the best portions of the Declaration of Independence by flickering candlelight as a dim sun struggled against the morning mist. If it was difficult, if it was important, Jefferson did it first.

If you want success, don't dawdle; don't pussyfoot. Hit those books early; then relax and have fun. Plow under your biggest weeds in the morning. Hold your "impossible" conference before the midmorning coffee break. Close your toughest deal by 8:30 in the morning. Make a list of all your tasks for the day. Do the hardest one first, and the others will seem easy. People will marvel at how much time you have for recreation and fun. When your hardest and most important jobs are all out of the way, you will play tennis or go on vacation without wrinkles on your brow. By completing the hardest tasks first, it's easy to be a success.

Start Your Tasks Early and Quickly

Some people, like cold engines, are slow starters. They have to warm up before anything happens, and by then usually all they get is sluggish performance. Be a fast starter. Don't procrastinate.

It is said that Daniel Webster applied to a law office for an apprenticeship. The instructions told applicants to arrive at 10:00 in the morning. Webster arrived at 9:00; three others arrived at 10:00, and one at 10:15. Who got the job? Daniel Webster, of course. Not only did he get the job. He continued to be an early starter and became a great leader in our country.

Charlie Glen and Levi Florey were Kansas wheat farmers. Each had 160 acres of ripening wheat. Glen repaired and tested his combine harvester until it was smooth and humming. Florey played some pool, fiddled around, and started late on his combine repair. It was not ready on Monday morning when the wheat was fully ripened. Charlie Glen was in the field cutting wheat at daybreak on Monday and finished Tuesday afternoon with 5,600 bushels of grain in his bins. Levi Florey finally got his machine repaired, and cut one swath of wheat Tuesday evening. That night a killer hailstorm swept across both places and there was no more wheat to harvest.

Neil Armstrong started his training early and became an honor student at USC, long before there was any chance to set foot on the moon. Because he started early, he was ready. He was chosen.

He made that one great stride as an astronaut and a giant leap for mankind.

Start early: succeed. Start late: fail. The choice is yours.

Strive for Excellence, Not Perfection

Use your time to improve your performance every single day, and be satisfied with steady growth. Set goals that will take a lifetime to approach and that will never be fully achieved. Your success and happiness will accompany the process of self-improvement, rather than arriving at true perfection and trying to remain happy thereafter.

Alexander the Great sought to be the perfect warrior. He fought his way across Greece, Asia Minor, Egypt, and into every other civilized country. Then, with an empire stretching from the Adriatic Sea to India, he sat down and cried because there were no more worlds to conquer.

At the University of Colorado, they called Tim Hunter "The Brain." He was an A student. On a 100-point exam, he would sometimes get 95 or 97. This bothered Tim and sent him back to the books. He worried over the 5% errors, rather than glowing over the 95% correct answers. He could never quite make that perfect 100, so one evening after a tough exam in Chemistry II, he went home and gulped a bottle of sleeping pills.

A young attorney in Houston left his law practice to get rich in real estate. He bragged that he would have $5 million before he was 40. He actually hit the five million mark, helped by inflation, late in his 38th year. Then he plunged into high-risk speculations for $10 million. He overworked, lived on coffee and cigarettes, drank too much, and lost half of his $5 million.

He wanted too much too fast. At 43 his hands trembled, he was divorced, his two boys avoided him, and he looked on himself as a failure.

Success lies in excellence. Achieve a small objective each week, month, or year. Keep moving toward your goal and enjoy the trip. You don't have to be perfect. No one is perfect. If you never quite make it, enjoy the view from *near* the top of your mountain.

Enlist the Support of Others

Your time span on this earth greatly determines the degree of success that you can achieve. If your ancestors had longevity, if you live a healthful life in a healthful environment, and if you're lucky, you can stretch that time span like a rubber band and have more years for achievement, maybe beyond that three score and ten. I write this looking back from age 99.

Because your time has an unknown limit, you may not progress far toward your goal if you have to wade through continuous resistance from others. Instead of having people slow your progress, enlist their help. If your goal is worthwhile, others will want to travel in that direction, too. People are gregarious. They want to travel together.

First, work with your family. Then enlist support in your community. That's the way it is done in churches, schools, city hall, the Red Cross, service clubs, unions, and political parties.

Cain and Abel could not work together, and so only Cain survived. A family divided against itself has little hope for success. A warring neighborhood will not enjoy great civic improvements. This country almost drowned in the blood of its own Civil War, but now we have achieved great strength through union.

If you wish to make more money, enjoy better vacations, improve your education, advance in your chosen career, enjoy better health, or win friends, then work with your brothers and sisters, your parents, your spouse. Remember that your span of time is limited, and you will move faster toward your goal when you have the assistance of others.

When you work, study, or play with others, you not only advance faster, but also you enjoy it more and help them, too. This is the essence of success.

TIPS FOR SUCCESS

- Don't procrastinate.
- Plan ahead.
- Form good habits; break bad ones.
- Ask for help when you need it.
- Take pride in your work.
- Learn to relax.

Schedule Periods of Rest or Changes of Activity

Before "industrial psychologists" and "organizational psychologists" began to counsel in business and industry, the workers in a Pittsburgh iron and steel company asked for and got brief rest periods. Instead of carrying heavy ingots of steel continuously, half the workers were allowed 30 seconds of rest after each load. The other half carried the ingots continuously. The company was surprised and very pleased to find that the brief-rest workers carried a significantly greater tonnage of steel each day than they had under the old scheme.

Winston Churchill was the lone leader resisting Hitler's Nazis before the United States was thrust into World War II by Pearl Harbor. His phone rang at all hours; he counseled, scrambled through bombed-out London rubble, studied maps, wrote speeches, and gave orders. Never was so much required of just one defender. Churchill wrote later that the way he got the most out of himself was to rest briefly between strenuous periods of work. He would work into the early hours of the morning, take a short nap, and work again.

Horses that run long distances will finish in better shape if given brief rest periods. Pioneers on the Oregon Trail soon learned that their teams of horses and oxen would hold up better if given rest periods, preferably at some good water hole.

Students have found in experimental psychology laboratories that a bent finger lifting a weight at the end of a string will fatigue and fail to function unless given needed rest periods. They also discovered that with brief rest periods, they could solve mathematical problems over extended periods with little drop in efficiency.

Relief from the grind is what vacations are all about. A few days away from a demanding job, or sometimes just a half-day off for recuperation, can work wonders. Often a few scattered short vacations may be better than long, extended vacations that often turn into drudgery themselves. The harried businessman who takes no exercise should not rush out every other week to make it all up with 18 holes of golf.

For successful performance, it is better to spice your work with many shorter periods of rest or exercise than with one longer break. The coffee break is industry's answer to this psychological need. When you start to lose concentration when trying to solve a problem, studying your notes or reading a textbook, get up and walk around a bit. Do not let the work become unconsciously associated with lack of concentration.

Stay on Track: Refuse to Be Interrupted

A little boy on his way to school rattles a stick along a picket fence, kicks a can, romps with his dog, stops to smell a flower, picks up a frog, and is late to class. He is not goal-oriented. In fact, he cares little for a goal and a track that someone else has set for him. He lacks motivation. There are two general types of motivation: intrinsic and extrinsic. An example of extrinsic motivation is what happens to the girl who wants to do well in her spelling tests because she wants to please her teacher. There is nothing wrong with that idea, but an even more powerful brand of motivation is operating when little Shirley wants to do well in spelling because her self-esteem calls for her best.

That's intrinsic motivation. Intrinsic motivation is best when we want to do something as well as possible. In the absence of these two types of motivation one sees aimless, unproductive wandering.

Most teenagers have vaguely jelled goals. They need counseling help in firming them up. Some people mature early, and others even reach middle age with hazy purposes. But when the goals are definite, then the successful person will stay on target.

Avoid the mistake of the wolfhound that switched trails and ended up chasing a field mouse. Keep your goal in focus. Plan time to travel toward it.

Jane has to make a B average to get into graduate school. Afternoons are sunny and nice. The phone rings, and Betty wants to go for a snack and a cappuccino. There's the unread morning paper. And how about Friday's party at the Big House? Interruptions, distractions, or graduate school? Which will Jane choose? Which will make for success?

Successful college athletes get tempting offers from professional football teams. They should choose to finish their degrees before turning professional. Success in later life is more likely with a college degree, earned by staying on track, avoiding interruptions and tempting offers.

Research workers at the United States Air Force base at Akron, Ohio, have soundproof rooms where light and temperature are held constant. They avoid disruptions and stay on track. The scientists at Rockefeller University who discovered the double helix of DNA stayed on track.

For your own success, stay on that straight track. Advance toward that important goal, then take time off to read the daily newspapers or a mystery story. Shoot your total energy straight as an arrow, and success is yours. The old axiom of Ben Franklin, "a stitch in time saves nine," is true and not just for sewing. Never put off for tomorrow what you can do today. Then rest tomorrow!

Finish Strong: Complete Your Task

Bruce Jenner won the decathalon in the Olympics at Montreal because he finished strong in every event. Other contestants led in the early going, but Bruce Jenner forged ahead at the finish.

Students, actors, salesmen, housewives, and farmers have to finish strong. In many colleges half the freshmen never finish a four-year course. What good does it do a ballet dancer to practice for several years getting ready for the big night if he or she is going to "take it easy" for the final weeks? Salesmen who are easily discouraged never close the big deal. Homemakers can be all smiles in the morning but grumpy and rude to a hungry family in the evening. Then, there was that Iowa farmer who was the envy of his neighbors in preparing soil and planting, but he wasted harvest time and let the November rains ruin his ripened crop. It is the strong finish, be it in the final college course or the harvest that counts.

Remember that psychologically you have great potential. The world is yours. You have springs of power — potential — just waiting to be tapped and managed. Live the good, vigorous goal-directed full life and you cannot fail. In life, the person who perseveres is the person who has the best chance to win. The person who quits has no chance. This is all true. Great achievement is yours, and it all depends on you.

Leave Tomorrow's Worry at the Shop or Office

Remember how workers could carry more ingots of steel with spaced rest periods during the day? The same psychological principle holds true for longer periods of time, such as the week or the month. Students who work at the campus library and come home to worry into the wee hours of the morning will do poorly on tomorrow's multiple-choice test. Businessmen and -women who work until they are exhausted at five o'clock and then bring home a briefcase full of trouble will not be at their best the next day.

Solve your problems and lay them aside with a feeling of work well done. If you have a fuss with your spouse, resolve it. Give a little. Negotiate and compromise. Never let the sun set on ill will. Turn from negative disagreement to positive affection.

When you quarrel, worry, fret, fume, and fear, your digestion goes sour, sweet affection turns bitter, and fatigue leaves you hollow. When you relax, play, enjoy food and affection, laugh and "recreate," you are recharging your pools of hidden power. Tomorrow will be a fruitful day, a day of success.

It is said that Agamemnon, Julius Caesar, and Napoleon Bonaparte all fought with intense determination during the day, but at night they relaxed and made merry until the next morning's battle. They left their worries, fears, and torment behind — at least for the moment. General Dwight D. Eisenhower practiced this strategy and did not panic during the Battle of the Bulge.

Delight in Accomplishment . . . and Relax

Take stock each day of what you have accomplished — and then relax.

Do you need to learn how to relax? Try this technique. Relax your muscles. Envision the muscle fibers as a bunch of loose, limp rubber bands. If necessary, tighten and then relax each group of muscles, starting with your toes and going up and over the top of your scalp. Let the expression drop right off from your face. Let that feeling of relaxation go from your shoulders out through your fingertips and back down to your toes. Make the muscles around your eyes so loose and limp that you couldn't open them even if you wanted to.

Then, just as you have relaxed your body, relax your mind. See yourself in a favorite place, such as a park. You can imagine yourself there by yourself or with a favorite companion. Use mental imagery to see that favorite place. Smell the flowers. Feel the breeze on your skin. Hear the birds. Forget about the everyday worries. It is all right to leave behind the worries about all the work you have to do for a few well-deserved moments of true relaxation.

Stay positive. Enjoy your moments of relaxation, your evening meal, an active family, a good show, companionship, love and affection. The sun will come up tomorrow, and you will be under it — shining with success.

The miner who hates his diggings, the housewife who feels bothered by growing children, and the clown who tires of making people laugh are all headed for the shallows. But the office manager who enjoys working with papers and people, the teacher who loves teaching his or her subject to children, and the trucker who likes the road will all find happiness — and experience less stress during their hours at work.

Most of our time is spent on the job. If we deeply dislike our work, then no amount of fun and games will add up to deep enjoyment. Life will be a drag.

For work to be enjoyable, it must be successful work. No one revels in failure. D's and F's are not the stuff of celebration. Rotting vegetables on a stalled truck and deficits on the author's report are not hilarious. Real pleasure comes with a feeling of accomplishment. A profitable bottom line, the landed fish, and a new invention — these are exciting.

A Vietnam prisoner of war I met sought and got a job as a forest ranger. He said, "I tried sailing, golf, tennis, and spectator sports, but the hell and horror of Hanoi's prison haunted me by day and erupted into screaming nightmares by night. But two months up here in these Washington woods . . . I'm at peace, with a dimming memory."

Carlyle said, "A man is composed into a kind of real harmony the instant he sets himself to work."

Happiness is not an end in itself, but it accompanies work and accomplishment. If your work is dull and never-ending, happiness fades. But with completion, with "closure," as the Gestalt psychologist would put it, there is the joy of satisfaction. Stanhope, Earl of Chesterfield, said, "Accomplishments give luster." The eminent psychologist, Louis P. Thorpe of the University of Southern California, said that even a child needs to experience achievement: the need to keep "doing more" and "doing something better."

Since happiness accompanies accomplishment, it can be enhanced by greater accomplishments. Taking the time to enjoy those accomplishments, rather than belittling the achievement and rushing wildly into another project, can also enhance happiness. Happiness is habit-forming. Let yourself be happy. Allow yourself to enjoy achievement. This approach, psychologically, will build greater power in your life.

Repeated intervals of happiness accompanying successful achievement are the greatest use of time. This reinforcing accomplishment with happiness builds personal power.

Things to Do

Time is all you have, intervals of time. During these intervals you have to achieve your life's goals. Time is money. Time is a successful career. Time is a happy interpersonal and romantic life. Time is a spiritual thread that links you to your faith. Following are some activities that can help you think about time and use it well.

1. Draw a straight line from Year 1 to as many years as you hope to expect to live. Write your life's goals on the line. For example, in what year do you expect to graduate from high school, college, advanced training? When will you get the next promotion or attain peak performance? Chart your projected milestones and goals.

2. Study successful people. How did they make use of the 10 rules for better use of time.

3. When you have a lesson to learn or a job to do, time your efforts from beginning to completion. How might you have done the task better and in less time?

4. Draw a vertical line down the middle of a sheet of paper. On the left side, write ways of using time that lead to failure. On the right side, write ways of using time that lead to success. Which side of the sheet do you fall on?

CHAPTER NINE

How to Manage Money

Money is power. Money represents a predetermined value that can be exchanged for the things we need and want. Money is neither good nor bad in a moral sense. It's the way in which one uses money that counts.

Money is the medium of exchange that is made, saved, or spent during our intervals of time. You need money to live. In this complex civilization, it is impossible for you to grow all of the food, mine the minerals, and manufacture all of the supplies, equipment, and tools that you need. All of these can be obtained or purchased with money.

Use your money wisely and you will be happy and successful. Use it to improve your health, education, career, and recreational enjoyment. Use it to help others in the same way. If you misuse your money, you can destroy a reputation, lessen your pleasure in living, and ruin your relationships with family and friends. Properly used, and put to work, money can be your golden key to the good life. Benjamin Franklin said, "If a man empties his purse into his head, no man can take it away from him." An investment in knowledge always pays the best interest.

Money and You

Do you want to be a millionaire? Why not? Remember your hidden powers. To be or not to be a millionaire is your choice. Psychologically, you have the power. Develop it. Set your goal, and never slow or deviate from the pathway. You'll make it. How do you think Charles Schwab, Andrew Mellon, Howard Hughes, John D. Rockefeller, Joseph Kennedy, Paul Lucas, Bill Gates, and

Frank Winfield Woolworth became millionaires? They did the right things to make money. You can do them, too. To be a millionaire, all you have to do is be a compulsive saver and a perpetual investor.

It was in 42 B.C. that Publilius Syrus said, "Money alone sets all the world in motion." You, too, can set your part of the world in motion with the power of your money.

Just over two thousand years after Publilius Syrus, it was Albert Einstein, when asked by a student, "What is the greatest power on earth?" "The greatest power?" answered Einstein. "Compound interest!"

It is easy to make money, hard to save, and most difficult of all to invest wisely. A fool and his money are quickly parted, but the wise person uses it for greater success and satisfaction. Some have said that money cannot buy happiness, but those very same people use it to buy the miseries they experience.

The year that I was born, the Dow-Jones average was 64. In June 1999, *U.S. News & World Report* listed the Dow-Jones above 11,000. The same issue told the story of Audrey Schaefer, a 38-year old mother in Maryland who "took control of her portfolio and now earns annual returns of 35 percent." She followed Einstein's law of compounding.

Never in any age has it been so easy to be rich. Never in any country has it been so easy to accumulate wealth. Your time and place for moneymaking is now. The poor sharecropper, the child of the ghetto, the orphan on the wrong side of the tracks, all revel in opportunities that were not available to the peons, serfs, and slaves of other times, whose odds of climbing the economic ladder were zero. Thanks to free education and the elimination of class barriers, each American can earn a chosen place on the economic scale. This now is truer in other industrial, democratic countries as well. Press your economic accelerator! You'll be there.

10 Rules for Effective Money Management

The vehicle to your personal fortune does not offer a free ride. Good money management is not automatic. It is not easy. You must adhere to some commonsense rules. Following are 10 rules for effective money management.

1. Start investing as early as possible.
2. Save and invest, rather than hoping for a higher salary.
3. Keep investments nearby and under your control.
4. Make money work for you (á la Einstein) by using the power of compound interest.
5. Buy, but seldom sell, real estate.
6. Pay your debts and taxes first.
7. Avoid credit card interest by paying the full balance.
8. Don't rely just on a retirement plans.
9. Buy what you need instead of what you want.
10. Feel rich in proportion to the things you can get along without.

Start Investing Early

Legend has it that Native Americans sold Manhattan Island for $24. Historically, the Manhattan Indians sold the island in 1626 to the Dutch West India Company. Since then, the value of that chunk of soil has increased some.

Ever since the Pilgrims landed at Plymouth Rock, all you have needed to do to make money is to buy and hold real estate. Ninety percent of the millionaires of America have made their fortunes directly or indirectly through lands, buildings, and factories. Lands flowing with milk and honey, deserts of sand and gold, the fruited plains, are all expressions of the beneficence of Mother Earth. If you want to be rich, get title to some of this real property and soar skyward on its magic carpet.

Will Rogers once reminded folks, "They're makin' more people, but not makin' more land." The supply of land is constant, and the demand keeps going up. If you cannot buy real estate, try stocks, bonds, annuities, treasury bills, or other securities. Mutual funds can help you, but use caution, as I'll explain elsewhere. Check performance of the fund you are considering in journals such as *Consumer's Reports*. Go for no-load funds over those that charge fees and commissions.

Basically, there are two kinds of purchases: those that appreciate and those that depreciate. Real estate, securities, and savings accounts are examples of those that appreciate. But household furniture, automobiles, and clothing represent purchases that depreciate.

Because time is money, if you want to become wealthy, start your economic program with your first dollar. Save some, as much as you can, and don't hide it under the mattress. That's burying your talents. Inflation will erode its worth. Invest that money and make it earn more money for you. If you are young, you may choose higher risk and higher possible earnings. But if you are older, you may choose lower risk and more secure investments.

In all cases begin your investments early, but if you have let opportunities pass you up, it is never too late to begin. Time is on your side. Start now. Suppose, for example, that you are 10 years old, and Granddad gives you $10. You can spend those $10 on a movie and popcorn, so tomorrow you have nothing. Or suppose you make an investment that will earn you 10% per annum compounded annually. When you are forty, you will have $198.37. When you are seventy, you will have $3,935.22, all from that ten-dollar bill that you almost blew on popcorn. So start early and let your money work for you.

When Benjamin Franklin said that a penny saved is a penny earned, he was most conservative. Suppose that in 1727, when he was 21 years old, he had invested that one penny at 8% compounded annually. His heirs would have $14,388,333.34 in the year 2001.

Save and Invest

You can never build a fortune from your salary. Ninety-five percent of people increase their standard of living as their salary advances. If you wish to make money, you dare not keep spending the total of your salary check. Try saving 10%. Save more if at all possible.

A recent author told how to make a million dollars in eight years. He did it himself. He made the million by buying apartments and pyramiding his investments. But he said that his almost impossible obstacle was saving the first $500.00 for a down payment. After that, it was easy. It takes money to make money.

If you are going to be a millionaire, you'll have to save and skimp. You must get that down payment. You must get money working for you. A raise in salary does not help if you spend it on items with decaying or disappearing values. To make money work for you, you need leverage. You can get leverage by saving or borrowing. If you save, you may have to do without a daily paper, miss movies and shows, walk instead of drive, wear your clothes another year, and buy healthy food in bulk instead of unhealthy fast food. You will not only save, but you may have better health and enjoy the satisfaction of success.

Another way to get leverage is to borrow. But you have to pay interest. This may eat up most of your earnings. Borrowed leverage has sometimes worked for real estate, but it would never work for deposits in your bank or credit union. So save your money. Invest it. Make it work.

Keep Investments Nearby and Under Your Control

Investments require management. If your property is geographically remote, you may be forced to hire a local manager. But almost never would a hired manager handle the property as well as you would.

Nearby personal management is what makes real estate one of your best investments. You can own the land that you farm, the house that you live in, a lot in your block, or a store in your town. You are right there. You can give your property the care that it needs. As an example of how absentee ownership can be damaging, a St. Paul businessman bought a grapefruit orchard in Florida. The week before his own packinghouse was to pick the fruit, an unknown group of pickers stole his whole crop.

Another example of remoteness and lack of control is ownership of securities. You may own a piece of U.S. Steel, Westinghouse, a package of bonds, or a mutual fund. In such investments you have relinquished control. Yes, you as a shareholder can vote, but for what? Usually for a board member that management has chosen. It is about as useless as buying passage on a vacation cruise tour to Jupiter. The corporate structure in America is not set up to properly represent you as a shareholder. This condition is not a subversive plot against you; it is just an intrinsic weakness of the system. For this reason, sound securities can be good, but not perfect investments.

Partnerships are often fraught with problems, for the minute you take in a partner, you have given up half of your control — and you are responsible for your partner's mistakes and misdeeds. If strict ground rules are drawn, partners can strengthen each other. But be cautious. Keep as much control as you can. The worst examples of the partnership principle are investment clubs and communes. They consistently fail. On the other hand, a successful partnership is Ernest and Julio Gallo. They started with a little grape patch and developed one of the best wineries in the world.

You already have the potential for management. Improve your control by study and practice. Learn about comparative values, purchase contracts, commissions, escrows, contingencies, title insurance, liens, purchase privileges, options, trust deeds and mortgages, notes, trusts, conversions, prepayment penalties, balloon payments, lease agreements, and the like. Be your own manager, your own boss, and your own captain: lord of all your surveyed property.

Stay close to your store, factory, farm, corporation, or mine. Manage and control your own investments. You will make them successful.

Make Money Work for You

Tip Fairbanks was a city engineer drawing $55,000 a year. He and his wife had three small children and owned a house worth $250,000 with a $25,000 mortgage. The neighbor next door needed money and would sell a $50,000 trust deed (mortgage) drawing 10% interest per annum at a discount of 25%, or for

$37,500. Tip and his wife knew that the mortgaged property was worth much more than $50,000. So they secured a $37,500 mortgage on their own home, paying 10% interest, and bought the neighbor's trust deed.

Why did Tip and his wife buy the neighbor's trust deed? By getting the 25% discount, they would eventually get $50,000 for $37,500, a capital gain of $12,500. Also, by paying 10% and getting 10%, the discount actually increased their interest yield to 13⅓%. In dollars and cents, it meant that they were making $1,250 in interest each year just by a paper transaction.

Tip and his wife noted this increase in annual income from a salary of $55,000 to $56,250. They decided against a new car that Tip wanted and invested the $1,250 in high-yielding treasury bills, at 9% per annum. This they would do every year. Because they were only 30, they calculated the result of 40 years of compounding and were shocked at the amount of money they would have at age 70 — just by letting the money work for them through the years: $422,353.06!

You, too, can make money work for you. Study. Draw a plan. Put it to work and keep it working.

TIPS FOR SUCCESS

- Never gamble. Save and invest instead.
- Invest wisely: diversify.
- Pay debts and taxes first.
- Shop carefully.
- Buy what you need, not just what you want.
- Pay off credit cards in full; avoid high interest.
- Buy real estate as an investment.

Buy, But Seldom Sell, Real Estate

Real estate. What is it? It is land, above and below the surface, and everything that people build on it. It represents three-fourths of all the wealth in this country. Do you own your share? Why not?

Start with home ownership. Why pay rent? That's pouring money down a black hole. It's gone. But your home will increase in value.

In the long run, real estate always does. It goes up, and up, and up. As soon as you have your home payments under control, buy some income property. Be a squirrel. Pack as much real estate as you can into your nest of security. That's financial success.

In addition to financial success, real estate ownership gives you added psychological strength. Maybe this is more important. Homeowners tend to be more settled, more stable, more contented. Would you like to plant your very own tree? Raise radishes and strawberries? You can't do that in a rented townhouse. But you are boss in your own backyard.

Real estate ownership improves your self-image. You come to believe that you are more important — and you are! Your territorial limit does not stop at the toe of your shoe but goes clear to the back fence, maybe all across a Wyoming ranch. You are an expanded personality. You are a greater person, with justifiable pride of ownership.

In addition to personality fulfillment, the landed gentry have always had higher social status. Does the homeowner seem more stable to you than the apartment renter? Bankers who approve risk loans think so.

It is patriotic to buy a home, or land, or a factory? Yes, the person who invests in this country supports it. You are less ready to tear the place down if you own some of it. Youngsters who own nothing are more radical. Older persons who have accumulated property tend to be more conservative. Maybe your love for this country is proportional to the amount of it that you own. Homeowners are not arsonists.

Yes, carefully buy, but seldom sell, real estate. You will benefit financially and psychologically. You will be a greater success with real estate than you will without it.

Pay Your Debts and Taxes First

If you want to build up credit, pay your debts when they are due. Better yet, pay them before they are due. When you build a habit of paying your debts early, your credit rating will be high;

and the banker will grant you another loan. Additionally, you will save a fortune in accrued interest.

Remember that money is power. You need money to work for you. The way to get it is to build your credit. Give your lender reason to trust you.

Unfortunately, many people spend their salary checks and forget that the debt and tax portion is actually not theirs to spend. They have filched their lenders' or the government's portion. They have spent another's money for their own wants. Sooner or later, these people come to grief and failure. They are the ones who worry because bankers do not trust them. Then they blame the banker and end up in economic chaos.

Play it square. "Render unto Caesar the things that are Caesar's." You will respect yourself. Those with whom you do business will respect you. You will enslave your borrowed dollars, and you will be a financial success.

Avoid Credit Card Interest by Paying the Full Balance

It's hard to pay in cash, but easy to charge. Just remember that sooner or later you will have to pay the bill. A majority of Americans use credit cards and end up paying 18% or more in interest on an unpaid balance. That's silly. It's economic lunacy. It's the road to financial catastrophe. If you cannot be sensible enough to use your credit cards moderately (that means paying the debt immediately, before service charges and interest accumulate), then throw them away. Pay cash and you will know better how much you are pouring down the drain. Remember, those revolving charge accounts are loaded — and not in your favor. Pay that bill as soon as it arrives.

The one exception to paying cash is investment in money-earning properties. This expenditure is leverage and makes sense if the money invested earns more than it costs you in interest. But for depreciating items such as the Porsche or fancy clothes, pay cash and weigh the cost.

Running up unwarranted debts for consumer goods is not only poor personal business, it is your contribution to setting up the country for a recession. The Great Depression of the 1930s started after reckless spending of borrowed money ("margin") overused the money supply. Prices had to fall.

U.S. News & World Report of 28 May 1979 commented on "The Shaky Pyramid of Consumer Debt." The article warned of recession because personal debt rose from $405 billion in 1968 to $1,364 billion in 1979. The recession did follow in 1980. Then it happened in 1990 and later years. Personally and nationally, too much debt is dangerous. When it gets too high, the whole house of cards comes tumbling down. Before this happens, kill the cancer of high consumer interest: Pay cash. Buy only what you can afford. Then the specter of the interest collector will not spoil your sleep, and you will be a successful money manager.

Don't Rely Just on a Retirement Plan

Many people believe that their retirement plan will provide enough money for their last years. It probably won't.

The two chief reasons that you will end up in financial misery if you depend solely on your retirement plan are: 1) people are living longer and 2) inflation can consume fixed buying power at a spiraling rate.

In addition, older people tend to need more medical and personal help. This takes extra money. Ezra Poundhammer retired as a dockworker in 1970 and believed that his union pension fund would keep Mary and him for life. Ezra had been lucky: no doctor bills. But maybe he will be lucky enough to be "unlucky" and outlive the real value of his pension. Even if he and Mary die early, they are already in trouble. When they went to the supermarket in Houston, they reported that it cost "three times as much for hamburger in 2002 as it did in 1970." Probably Ezra was conservative in that statement. If inflation soars, as it did during the Carter Administration (when there was double-digit inflation), those who depend on a fixed income could be in real trouble.

Use your retirement plan only as a supplement. Be independent. Put aside something for that inevitable rainy day. Invest. Build a capital fund. Buy annuities, low-risk stocks or bonds, life insurance, and, of course, real estate.

Trust in your own personal retirement plan, not in an organized retirement plan. Have you ever heard of an employee being fired at 55 and losing most of his or her retirement benefits? Could Social Security be under-funded? Yes! Congress sees the problem getting worse. Could someone get a hand in the retirement cookie jar? Even if none of these things happen, you are still better off being provident.

You can sleep tight when you have the secure feeling of knowing that your retirement check is nice, but unnecessary. Be proud of yourself for building an estate instead of blowing it all on Saturday night. Leave something when you are gone for the people and causes that are near and dear to you. Be a senior giver, not a senior starver. Feel the joy of successful use of those hidden powers and for leaving your economic world a little better place than when you found it.

Buy What You Need Instead of What You Want

About 90% of the people buy items on impulse. It looks good. They buy it. Stores place counters of impulse items between the customer and the cashier. They know you're gullible, and they harvest you. They're smart. Are you?

Magazines, candy, gum, an extra bracelet, a social climber's club, keeping up with the Joneses — is that what you need or just want? If you want it enough, buy it — and watch it turn to ashes.

Are you better off physically, mentally, socially, or personally when you buy an item? If you are, the item makes sense. You *need* it. But if it contributes to nothing more than a passing fancy, then you just *want* it. Buying it would be a foolish thing to do.

What are the real values of life? You need to look at your long-term goals now. Will buying an item bring you closer to those goals? Will it lengthen your life or improve your present living?

When you furnish your house, make a list of the needed items. Don't go to a furniture or home electronics store and just look around or, worse yet, let some eager salesman unload a jumble of misfits on you. Take time to shop around for the best buy. Consult consumer-oriented periodicals, such as *Consumer Reports.* Beware of phony claims that the product is rated number one in a less-than-honest periodical with a title that sounds like a legitimate consumer-oriented publication. Take advantage of coupons, specials, and other offers that put you more in control of a purchase. Avoid extended warranties like the plague! When you do the weekly grocery shopping, make a list and stick to it. Buy what you need and resist the ploy of those who want to sucker you out of your money.

When you limit buying to what you need, rather than what you want, and certainly not what the storekeeper "wants" you to buy, you will have extra money to invest. Money will work for you, your retirement will be secure, and people will respect you as a business success. You will have money for worthy causes and feel the pride of service. That makes good sense — and dollars-and-cents success.

Feel Rich in Proportion to the Things You Can Get Along Without

Attitudes govern your spending habits. If you feel rich, you are not tempted by baubles. It is easy to save when you have no desire to spend. With such an attitude, you will buy no more when you have $100 in your pocket than you do when you have only $10.

Psychologically, people are happiest when they feel that "the best things in life are free." The showy trinkets may be eye-catching but yield little in the way of a permanent satisfaction. Some who are insecure personally try to feed fallen egos on a diet of flash and sparkle. The purchase of such ego-boosting items is a temporary opiate, but trinkets, whether diamonds or Porches, do not fill the psychological needs of permanence and depth.

Those who have taken the effort to invest in good education, established worthwhile goals, improved human relationships, and developed a satisfying faith have little use for ego-boosting trinkets. They are concerned more with the basics of food, clothing, shelter, free enterprise, and other necessities that make life better for themselves, their families, their neighbors, and their country.

Suppose we sum up by saying: Successful and blessed is the person who is happy with necessities rather than being unhappy with the lack of imagined luxury.

Things to Do

Your personal power is extended with money. With money you can live better and help others to live better, too. You can make it. You can be a millionaire if you really want to. You must pay the price. But making a million now is easier than it ever has been. Following are some activities that can help you think more about how to manage your money.

1. Set moneymaking goals. How much net worth do you wish to have when you are 30, 40, 50, 65, 90?
2. How much will you save each week, month, and year? Establish a place for accumulation, whether in a savings account, a credit union, an annuity, or a mutual fund.
3. Study all investment possibilities: now, 10 years hence, 20, 30. Invest your savings in ways that take into account the long term.
4. Calculate the advantages and disadvantages of borrowing to invest. What net profit can you make?
5. Apply tax consequences to all of your investment plans. What will give you the highest yield after taxes?
6. Money, land, stocks, and corporations are yours only for your lifetime. Who will get them when you are gone? Should you: make a will; consider trusts to avoid probate; give to family and charities; and use life insurance to pay estate taxes? Make your plans now.
7. Study tax exemptions, deductions, credit deferments, and reporting. Gear your future investments to the tax structure.

8. Set down the ways in which moneymaking, saving, and spending will yield most to your physical, mental, personal, and social well-being, and to your financial neighbor as to your financial self.

CHAPTER TEN

Your "Points to Ponder" Checklist

Now that you know how to use your hidden powers for success, you will be more successful if you concentrate your thinking and your behavior on the most pertinent points of this book. Following are 10 *points to ponder*. Review them often and check your progress. Arrange your successes like the steps of a ladder, each one leading to, and becoming the means of, a higher success.

✔ 1. Discover and improve your vast reservoir of untapped, hidden powers.

✔ 2. Begin with attitudes of wanting to succeed. *Will* your success — and watch your persistent willpower carry you to success after success.

✔ 3. Of the billions of people, living and dead, *you* are utterly unique. No one is, or ever has been, like you. Your capabilities are one of a kind and can be sharpened and improved. Draw on your hidden capacities for success.

✔ 4. Never let the sun set on stagnant abilities. Learn, learn, learn. Hone each sword of your strength to its finest cutting edge.

✔ 5. Build psychological habits of success. Repeat your winning attitudes. Think of yourself as a winner. See yourself as a winner in your mind's eye. Prethink, think, and rethink the positive attitudes that lead you to greater and greater successes. Success begins in the mind, leads to action, and results in accomplishment.

✔ 6. If you would manage things and people, first manage yourself. Self-discipline is essential to success. Discipline every conscious moment toward your goal of success. Control and guide your mental, emotional, physical, social, and spiritual processes toward your chosen goals. Your hidden springs of power will take you there. Know it can happen, believe it can happen, see it happen.

✔ 7. Consider your environment. People, animal life, plants, earth, air, and water are waiting for your leadership and direction. You must help yourself and others by working in harmony with people and things about you. Manage well what you touch, and you will build a better world.

✔ 8. Time is a precious jewel. It is all you have. It is your life! Resolve to use time to the fullest. Use every precious moment to advance toward planned successes. Happy is the person who packs more worthwhile activity into every golden interval of time; miserable is the person who fritters it away.

✔ 9. Follow the 10 rules for money management, and you will be rich. Use your riches to satisfy your self-interest, and by mutual service satisfy the interests of others.

✔ 10. The psychology of success means shaping up your attitudes, initiating effective action, and enjoying fulfillment and success. Happiness is the partner of achievement.

Success is possible for you! As Professor David Bellman emphasized, "Don't even think the word *can't!*" Rub the genie's lamp of your hidden powers, marshal them, target your mind toward worthy goals, never give up, and great satisfaction will be yours.

ABOUT THE AUTHOR

Emery Stoops, Ed.D., observed his 99th birthday on 13 December 2001. *Psychology of Success* is his 18th book.

During his long career in education, Stoops has been a teacher, a counselor, an assistant principal, a principal, a superintendent, and a college professor. He also has been a member of Phi Delta Kappa for nearly 70 years, serving as its president from 1954 to 1956. He oversaw the relocation of PDK headquarters to its present site in Bloomington, Indiana.

Stoops is professor emeritus at the University of Southern California Rossier School of Education. In 1993 he received USC's Distinguished Emeritus Award. Stoops, with his wife Joyce, established the Emery Stoops and Joyce King Stoops Dean's Chair in the USC Rossier School of Education, the Emery Stoops and Joyce King Stoops Education Library, and 22 scholarships for Rossier School graduate students, among other gifts to the university.

Emery Stoops has served as a visiting professor at a number of institutions of higher learning, including the University of California at Los Angeles, the University of California at Berkeley, the University of Washington, the University of Alaska, the University of Denver, the University of Hawaii, the University of Pittsburgh, and New York University. He also served as a consultant for administrators in the Department of Defense schools in Germany, and as a consultant to the U.S. Office of Education, the California State Board, and to Riverside and Santa Barbara Counties.

When then-university policy required that Stoops retire at age 65, he was sought out as a board member of the San Francisco Life Insurance Company, later becoming the company's president and changing its name to Penn-Pacific Life. He became a California Licensed Agent for the sale of annuities, investment-type life insurance, IRAs, and mutual funds. Stoops took the advice he offers in this book: Never retire!

Stoops most recent previous book is a historical novel, *The Homesteaders*, which he published at age 98.